POPS

POPS

Learning to Be a Son and a Father

CRAIG MELVIN

wm

WILLIAM MORROW

An Imprint of HarperCollins*Publishers*

HarperCollins books may be purchased for educational, business,
or sales promotional use. For information, please email the
Special Markets Department at SPsales@harpercollins.com.

A hardcover edition of this book was published in 2021 by William Morrow,
an imprint of HarperCollins Publishers.

FIRST WILLIAM MORROW PAPERBACK EDITION PUBLISHED 2022.

Designed by Nancy Singer

Library of Congress Cataloging-in-Publication Data has been applied for.

ISBN 978-0-06-307200-8

22 23 24 25 26   LSC   10 9 8 7 6 5 4 3 2 1

CONTENTS

POPS

BEING THERE

M y father was born in 1950 in a federal prison in West Virginia. That is a heavy burden to carry into life, but he and I never talked about it, not for decades—not until I was forty-one, when I sat down to write this book. We never talked about why my grandmother had been imprisoned or for how long. We didn't talk about what, if anything, he remembered about her imprisonment, or who cared for him until she was released. We also didn't talk about his father's alcoholism, or the way his father squandered his life and nearly died alone. We didn't talk about how that legacy has affected him across his seventy years on this earth. We didn't talk about whether his father's problems contributed to his own alcoholism. We didn't talk about how his parents not being present probably led him to not being around as much as he wanted when he became a father to my two brothers and me. We didn't talk about what toll those absences took on his marriage to my mother, or why they stayed together when they had so many reasons not to.

We had a lot of ground to cover, my father and I. It took work and time, but we've come to a good place, and this book is the story of both our journeys to get there, separately and together. It's also the story of my larger family, and the love and faith that, despite some dark times and big obstacles, have bonded us through generations.

For me, part of this journey involved becoming a father myself. I have two children: my son, Delano, who's seven, and my daughter, Sybil, who's four. Being Del and Sibby's dad has made my life richer in ways I never could have imagined. Like most fathers, I have to juggle the responsibilities of parenthood along with the responsibilities of work, marriage, being a son and brother myself, and all the other roles and activities that make up a busy modern life. Sometimes it's hard. Often I feel like I've fallen short in one way or another. In fact, I've yet to meet the father or mother who doesn't feel that way.

All of which is to say that I now see my own father through a very different lens than I did when I was growing up in the 1980s and 90s in Columbia, South Carolina. Lawrence Melvin—Pops, to me— wasn't a "fun" drunk, if there even is such a thing. He could be mean. He was distant and antisocial. When his drinking got really bad, as it increasingly did when I became a teenager, his speech would slur, and more than once he threw up on himself while he was passed out in his bed. When he was home, he was usually in that bed, which was such a fixture of my childhood. He'd lie there watching sports, black-and-white episodes of *Perry Mason*, and Lifetime movies (yes, seriously). Mostly, though, he'd be watching his eyelids. Partly that was due to his drinking, but it was also a function of his job at the Columbia post office and the hours he worked as a mail clerk on the third shift—the graveyard shift.

That was a choice: you make a few more bucks when you work the third shift, but you sleep during the day. You get up in the afternoon, sometimes as late as six or seven in the evening. You go to work at ten or eleven at night. So in the mornings, when I would be heading off to school, Pops would be walking back in the door. This went on for the better part of my childhood. Consequently, he almost never made it to my Little League games. He wasn't around for most school events. He missed a lot of my childhood. Frankly, even when he was around, even when he was sober, he was often sullen and remote. I resented his absences and his emotional distance—and for years, even decades, I couldn't see past that.

Pops has two other sons—my older half brother, Lawrence, and my younger brother, Ryan. For a long time, the three of us didn't understand alcoholism—its crippling nature, the damage longtime alcohol abuse does to the brain. We blamed Pops. We assumed he was weak. We thought, *Pops is just a drunk. He could get his drinking under control if he really wanted to.* From my perspective, this was more or less a fact of life: I had a lousy dad. End of story.

But as I said, when you have your own children, you become more aware of the sacrifices fathers make to provide for their families. I began to see the toll living took on my dad: what he gave up; how things might have looked through his eyes while he worked a tough job with brutal hours to put food on our plates and a roof over our heads. I've also come to realize that Pops wasn't "just" a drunk. He was sick. He was an addict. He *is* an addict.

You can see that my feelings about my father and my childhood are complicated and that I'm still sorting them out. The same with my feelings about fatherhood in general. That's part of the reason I'm writing this book. At a basic level, my job as a journalist is to ask people questions and tell their stories; I've been doing that professionally for two decades now. But here I want to turn the camera around, as it were, and ask myself some tough questions, and ask my parents some tough questions, too, so that I can tell the stories of Lawrence and Craig Melvin, and what being fathers and sons has meant to both of us, as honestly and thoughtfully as I know how. To me, this book isn't a memoir; it's an investigation. The subject just happens to be personal.

ONE THING I'VE LEARNED AS A journalist is that every story—even your own—needs context. I can't say I planned things this way, but I've reported a lot of stories about family issues over the years, and since I've been on the *Today* show, I've done quite a few pieces focused on fatherhood. Is it possible I've been circling the subject as a subconscious way to understand my own history? I wouldn't argue the point.

Maybe most memorable for me was a story we did for the *Today* show in 2019 on Camp Grace, a program for fathers at Salinas Valley State Prison in Central California. This prison is a maximum security facility, housing over three thousand men; it's among the toughest prisons in the country. Many of the guys have been in for a while, and some of them are going to be in for quite a while longer. Many have been convicted of violent crimes—these aren't just street hustlers caught selling dime bags. But for five days every summer the prison hosts a day camp for inmates and their children, complete with crafts, games, dancing, and most important, the kind of quiet one-on-one time and physical contact that inmates and their families aren't allowed under normal visitation rules.

For the men, the price of admission is a year of good behavior. "This is a big incentive to do good," said Jonathan Badilla, an inmate convicted of attempted murder. I met him at Camp Grace with his two young children, Lailani and Jonathan Jr. "I feel very blessed to be here," Jonathan told me, his arms around both kids. As several of the other men explained, it's not that their children can't visit other times of the year, but when they do, it's usually with their mother or a grandparent or some other guardian, and the visits take place in a crowded, noisy, heavily guarded meeting room. The men never get one-on-one time with their kids behind bars. Camp Grace was a first.

Another dad I met had participated in the program for several years. He had a daughter in middle school. I'll never forget what he told me about Camp Grace: "You start just kind of playing, throwing the ball and doing arts and crafts. But then a couple of years in, you're starting to have those serious conversations with your preteen daughter, those awkward conversations about boys, about life, the birds and the bees, and who to trust. Conversations that fathers shouldn't be having with children behind bars."

The two women who started the program met in the prison's visiting room. They both had husbands who were incarcerated. The women's goal was to ameliorate the sad fact that children of inmates are punished alongside their dads by being denied any meaningful contact with them—truly a case of sons and daughters suffering for the sins of their fathers. Evan Freeman, another Camp Grace participant, who is incarcerated for bank robbery, made that point very eloquently to me. I talked to him while his son, Evan Jr., a bright-eyed but shy boy, clung to his waist. I asked Evan, "To those who would look at this and say, 'These guys, they don't deserve to have this kind of time with their kids,' what you would say to that?" (To be honest, I was similarly skeptical when my producer, Jared Crawford, first proposed the story to me.) Evan thought about it for a long moment, then said, "They're probably right. But my *kid* deserves to have time with me. Whatever the reason why we're here, we're still people. Our kids are still kids and they need their dads in their lives." I asked how he copes with the 360 days a year when he can't be in Evan Jr.'s life. "It's hard," he said twice, then added in a confidential tone, "Another thing that's fortunate for me is that I'm in a cell by myself now, so I can cry when I want to cry, you know?" His voice was breaking. Mine did, too.

Off-camera, I really lost it a couple of times talking to these men. They were more than willing to be interviewed—talking about their kids seemed cathartic for them. Frankly, I had started our day of reporting at Salinas Valley seeing these men solely as felons. Once I started talking to them, I realized, "Oh, wait a minute. This is a chapter in their story. It isn't the entire story. This is a part of who they are—not *all* of who they are." I started to connect with them as dads, as fathers who seemed to regret whatever terrible choice or series of terrible choices they had made to wind up inside. I know I've been very fortunate in a lot of ways, and at times I couldn't help thinking, "There but for the grace of God go I." Most of us take big risks and do dumb things when we're young. You know the kind of thing I mean: *that one night, had I turned left instead of right.* . . . I definitely made some bad choices earlier in my life, and sometimes when you're young the margin for error is extremely slim—especially when you're young and you look like me.

The more I talked to the men at Camp Grace, the more I realized that they're missing most of what it means to be a dad. They're missing all the milestones in their children's lives—the first steps, the first words, the first time on a bicycle without training wheels, Little League games, recitals, breakups, graduations—many of them will miss it all. What I was privy to at Camp Grace were some of the only memories that they're going to have of their children. It was heartbreaking. We were shooting there for only two days, so we weren't around for the goodbyes at the end of the week. I'm not sure I could have stood it anyway.

There is so much about fatherhood that many of us take for

granted. The little moments. My boy, Del, for instance, is going through a phase now where he likes to climb into bed with my wife, Lindsay, and me just about every night. And he doesn't simply climb in and interrupt my sleep. He sleeps like a child who has been possessed by some sort of satanic being: his arms start flailing about and hitting me in the face. And then, on top of that, he'll complain about how much space I'm taking up *in my own bed*. But the truth is, there have been any number of nights where I lie awake thinking, *You know, this is not that bad. There is going to be a time in my life where I am probably going to miss this.*

Of course, my dad missed a lot of those little moments. So did his dad. And when my dad was a boy, I'm sure the federal penal system didn't have anything like Camp Grace to help him to connect with his mother. I suspect that's part of the reason I found reporting that story so moving: the fact that members of my own family have been on both sides of that situation.

BEFORE IT AIRED, I WORRIED THAT the Camp Grace story wouldn't resonate with the *Today* show audience. My fear was that viewers wouldn't be able to see past these men's crimes and relate to them as fathers. But the positive response was tremendous. Since then, I've started a *Today* show series called "Dads Got This!," in which I've profiled dads across the country, individual men as well as groups of men. The common denominator is that these are dads who have had to meet challenges as they care for their children. Sometimes the stories are about more lighthearted hurdles, like the one on dads who have learned how to sew costumes for their daughters' dance squad or the piece on fathers who have taken on the sometimes-daunting job of doing their daughters' hair. Sometimes the stories are about more serious challenges facing fathers, like the group of mostly evangelical dads who have banded together to support their LGBTQ+ children while facing ostracism from their churches, or the father who channeled his grief after his daughter's death from a drug overdose into founding a clinic to treat young addicts.

Our viewers' response to the "Dads Got This!" series—from men as well as women—has been overwhelming and enthusiastic. People love seeing dads taking on unexpected roles and acing them. The truth is, even in an era where so many traditional assumptions about gender and family have been overturned, it can still feel as if fatherhood is defined by Ward Cleaver and Cliff Huxtable (or maybe Homer Simpson and Peter Griffin, depending on the era). There just aren't a lot of folks talking about all the different roles modern dads are taking on right now. Which reminds me of a Chris Rock bit, one of my favorites. It's the one where he talks about dads getting no love. Moms, he points out, are constantly getting showered with love and compliments—not that there's anything wrong with that—whereas the only thing dads get by way of a thank-you, as Chris says, is "the big piece of chicken." That's the love dads get: a breast instead of a wing. It's a joke that has stayed with me. While Chris is obviously exaggerating, he's not wrong.

Fathers need to be celebrated. I've been moved by so many of the dads I meet, their eloquence and emotion. Men don't generally talk a lot about what we do as husbands and fathers—it's sort of in the nature of manhood not to, at least traditionally. We don't talk about our kids who are sick or vulnerable, who are gay or trans, who have challenges, who are excluded by other kids for whatever reason. We also don't talk a lot about the satisfactions of raising our children, the pure joy. That's just not something that most men do. My dad barely talked, period. But the dads in our stories were laying it all out and forging deep emotional connections with their children and with other fathers. At the same time, without a lot of fuss or self-pity, they were taking care of what they thought needed to be done—like generations of American fathers before them, including Lawrence Melvin, who, despite his drinking problem, had one of the strongest work ethics I've ever known.

Another thing I've learned from the dads I've interviewed is to loosen up a bit. I tend to be pretty hard on myself, professionally and personally. As a father, I don't feel like I'm around as much as I want to be. With my *Today* show schedule, I'm usually at work when my kids are having breakfast and getting ready for school. (In that sense, I'm not so different from my dad, I have to confess, as painful as that admission is.) I worry that I don't have the same kind of emotional connection to my kids that my wife has. But as I've talked to other dads, I've realized we're all in the same boat. We all feel like we're falling short in some way: either we're not present enough, or we're not making enough money, or we're not setting a good enough example. But most of us are doing the best we can. That's true of the dads I've been interviewing. I hope it's true of me. This book is in part my effort to try and answer that for my own dad.

In 2018, when he was sixty-seven, Pops summoned up a strength and courage I didn't know he had to face down his demons—and his biology—to become sober. It was a game changer for our family. I'm going to be writing about some very tough times that we went through before that, including some episodes I wish I could forget. But there are good memories, too. Here's one I cherish. I played second base in Little League, and once, when I couldn't have been more than ten or eleven, I came up to bat and happened to look down the left-field line. Surprise: there was my dad, standing by himself, watching me. I don't recall his ever being at a game prior to that. But the night before I had said to him, "It'd be nice if you could make it to a game." I had said it kind of offhandedly. I was afraid to make too big a deal of it, but it was important to me, maybe more so than I knew at the time. And for once he heard me. That afternoon, when he normally would have been sleeping, he had showed up for me. I don't remember how I did or whether I got a hit or not. What I remember vividly—the important thing—was that he was *there*.

CHAPTER 1

WHERE I'M COMING FROM

When I sat down to talk with Pops for this book, I was surprised at how willing and open he was. Contrary to my fears, it was almost as if he'd been waiting quietly all these years for me to question him, even on painful subjects. Like his relationship with my grandfather.

I don't know a whole lot about Pops's dad, whose name was Curtis Amaker. And Pops never really talked about him. My understanding was always that they didn't have much of a relationship. According to my mother, her father-in-law spent much of his life, and certainly his later years, living in squalor and more or less drinking himself to death.

Given the disparaging way my mom has always talked about my grandfather, I'd never been all that curious about him. I did meet him once, when I was five or six years old. We were on a trip to New York City, where he lived at the end of his life, and either my mom or my dad presented him to me and said, "This is your grandfather. This is Grandpa Curtis." I remember thinking, *He looks old*. When you're five or six, anyone over the age of forty seems ancient, but even as a kid I could sense he wasn't in the best of health. He moved slowly and he had that old-man smell. I was struck by the fact that he looked like my dad. I don't think we said much of anything to each other.

Talking to Pops recently, I asked straight out what kind of relationship he'd had with his father. "None, none," he said. "I would go to see him after I got a little older, but you know, when I was just growing up and whatnot, he never did anything for me."

"So he made no effort?"

"Nope." Pops repeated the word several times, almost like he was registering the answer for the first time.

"Did he ever say why?"

"No, and I never did ask him, either."

It wasn't until Pops was eight or nine that he even learned Curtis Amaker was his father. Pops grew up in Cayce (pronounced *Kay-see*), a small city across the river from Columbia, where I was born. Curtis had been working for a lumber company located by the railroad tracks that cut through town. One day he was walking home along the tracks after work and saw Pops. He called my father over.

"We was talking," Pops said, "and I think he told me then that he was my daddy. 'I didn't know you was my daddy.' 'Yep.'"

"Before that," I asked, "who did you think your father was?"

He said that "at a certain age" he'd begun to wonder about it, but that for the most part he hadn't given the question all that much thought. "It's not like you and your kids. Sibby and Del know you're their daddy because you be there every day for them. Shit, as far as I knew, I didn't have a daddy. I was out there with nothing."

I asked if he'd gone to his mother to find out if what Curtis had told him was true.

"No."

"Why not?" I was more than a little incredulous.

"I don't know. I guess I wasn't interested."

"So you *never* asked her about it?"

"No, I never did. I was feeling that nobody wants to tell me, so I guess they don't want me to know, so I ain't going to ask."

I told him he would have been a terrible journalist, and we both laughed. I wondered if Curtis had subsequently tried to forge any kind of relationship with Pops, maybe given him a little money from time to time.

"No, he didn't. Shit, every time I saw him, I'd have to give *him* something."

"Oh, he wanted money from you?"

"Yeah. He was a deadbeat." He was also a wino, Pops said, and drank a lot more than even Pops did at the height of his own addiction.

I asked if Curtis had ever explained how he met Pops's mother.

"Nope, I don't know anything about that."

"You never asked?"

"Never asked."

"Did you not ask because you didn't want to know?"

"I don't know why. Like I said, back in them days, the grown folks would only tell you what they wanted you to know, and that was it. They didn't let the kids ask a bunch of questions. Back in them days, kids didn't hardly question their parents or whatnot. They just did what their parents told them to and kept on going."

CURTIS AMAKER CLEARLY DIDN'T MEAN MUCH to my grandmother, either. She had five kids with three different men, at least, and there was a sixth child who died at the age of a year or two. The reason listed on the death certificate was neglect or malnourishment. So there are some very dark corners in my family's history that up to now I've rarely tried to look into.

My mom recently found a copy of a separation agreement between my grandmother, who was born Surena Richardson in 1917, and her first husband, Booker T. Melvin, who fathered her two oldest children, Carrie Mae and Bonnie Lee, and who passed his name onto my father and me. The agreement is dated August 1946, and split the two children between husband and wife, with my aunt Bonnie Lee going with her father and Carrie Mae staying with my grandmother. The agreement specifically states that Booker T. was "discharged from all obligation of alimony, or support," meaning that for all intents and purposes, Surena was a single mother—a challenge for anyone, anytime, but not least for a black woman in South Carolina in the late 1940s who only had a sixth-grade education. (That was essentially as far as the segregated local schools went when she was young.) She gave birth to my uncle James a year later, in 1946. My dad was born in 1950.

I didn't find out that the woman I knew as Grandma Rene (pronounced *Reen*) had been in prison until I was preparing for college. I needed my father's birth certificate for some registration form. I was double-checking that everything matched up with what I knew— birth date, parents' names, et cetera—when I noticed the listing for Pops's place of birth: "Alderson, West Virginia." I didn't recognize the town, but I thought, *West Virginia? We have no family in West Virginia.* It had never come up in any conversations with my parents. At that point in my life, I'd never even been to West Virginia. As far as I knew, no one in my family had.

So I asked my mom. And she told me, reluctantly: Grandma had been in prison when dad was born. She encouraged me to ask him about it, but I never did. Maybe I figured that he wouldn't really give me an answer, that he'd be evasive or clam up altogether. Maybe I was afraid he'd get mad. Maybe I simply didn't have the guts to ask him. Back then, Pops and I just didn't have those kinds of conversations. I could certainly see how he wouldn't want to open a vein on the subject. After all, if you're born in prison, that's probably not something you're proud of. I don't even know why or how my mom knew. She just said to me, "I've told you everything I know. If you want more, you're going to have to ask your dad."

And of course I had a lot of questions even if I felt I couldn't ask anyone. What was she in for? Did Grandma kill a man? If you were a woman in federal prison in the 1940s and 50s, you had to have done something pretty hard-core, especially if it was a first offense. What kind of life had she been living? I still can't get my head around how desperate she must have been as a single mom with young kids.

I've since learned that she was running numbers—my parents have some of her old notebooks keeping track of bets—and that she was also involved in some kind of bootlegging operation. The "Alderson" on my dad's birth certificate was a reference to the Alderson Federal Prison Camp, the first federal woman's prison, which opened in 1928 and was progressive for its day. In pictures, it looks almost like a New England prep school campus, and in the early days the women were housed in cottages with private rooms and were offered classes in subjects like sewing and knitting. As an "alumna," Grandma Rene is in interesting company: Billie Holiday spent a year in Alderson following her 1947 narcotics conviction, and Grandma served her time alongside Kathryn Kelly, the wife of the Prohibition-era gangster "Machine Gun Kelly," who was imprisoned for a 1933 kidnapping, and Iva Toguri D'Aquino, the Japanese-American woman commonly referred to as Tokyo Rose, who was convicted on dubious evidence of participating in Japanese propaganda broadcasts during World War II; President Gerald Ford would eventually pardon her. Later prisoners have included Sara Jane Moore and Lynette "Squeaky" Fromme, both of whom separately tried to assassinate Ford. Martha Stewart spent five months in Alderson in 2005 following her conviction on charges related to insider trading. (Stewart, by the way, has been a fixture on the *Today* show, going back forty years. I've sometimes thought of bringing up our Alderson connection when she's been on the show—and quickly thought better of it.)

I still don't know for what precisely Grandma Rene was convicted. When I finally brought up the subject with my dad, I said, "The scuttlebutt is that she was in for bootlegging and that it probably wasn't her first offense." He said, "Yeah, I always heard it was bootlegging, too, but honestly I don't know much more than that." He said he'd never asked his mother or his older siblings.

I asked him how he had found out that he was born in prison, and he had a story similar to mine: he discovered it when he needed his birth certificate for some reason. But he also said that from time to time when he was growing up, people had called him a "jail baby," which hurt him when he was old enough to understand what it meant.

I also talked to Uncle James, who said it was his understanding, too, that Grandma Rene had been convicted of bootlegging. He has vague memories of staying with relatives in North Carolina while she was in Alderson. (I wrote this book during the coronavirus pandemic, when federal archives that might still have Grandma Rene's records were closed.)

The funny thing is, while Grandma Rene's prison term was maybe a source of shame for my dad, I wish I'd known about it when I was younger. I could have bragged about it: "Hey, my grandma was a badass!" For a kid in the 1980s and 90s, it would have been a badge of honor. Who knows? Maybe grandma was a bootlegging kingpin.

Pops said he had memories of Grandma Rene selling illegal liquor out of her house *after* she'd been released from prison: "When I was in fourth, fifth, sixth grade, people used to come by and buy their little bootleg and sit in the back and drink it." She was a middleman, he said; someone brought the liquor to the house for her to sell, so if she had once been a kingpin, I guess she eventually scaled back a bit. Whatever her level of involvement, it was driven by her need as a single mother to support three young children: Pops, James, and their youngest brother, Charles. "I'd say I can count the times I seen Mama drinking some liquor," Pops told me. "Mama wasn't no drinker. She was selling it. What do you call that? Just doing something to survive, I guess."

Actually, the way I see it, Grandma Rene was an entrepreneur in an era when that wasn't an option for most women. I wish I'd had a chance to talk to her about all that—she died before I found out about her time in prison—but I doubt the conversation would have gone well. When I knew her, Grandma Rene was all Jesus, all the time—a truly God-fearing, churchgoing woman. Pops told me that by the late 1950s she had given up the liquor business and was working at a local dry cleaners while also cleaning houses for white people. As well, she had started attending church regularly. He couldn't remember any dramatic spiritual awakening on her part, though. As he pointed out, "Hey, you could find the Lord and still be a bootlegger."

I suppose there's an argument to be made that if you spend as much time as she had on the dark side, you probably need to spend a couple of decades trying to get right with God, and however much she had sinned before I was born, she was a saint when I knew her.

In her words and deeds, she gave no indication that she'd led any other kind of life.

When I was growing up, she lived in Cayce, in the same house my dad grew up in, and her days revolved around the Mount Pleasant Baptist Church, where she was an usher. She lived only a block away, so she would walk to and from church. Fortunately for my brothers and me, she was a New Testament grandmother, not an Old Testament grandmother. She never raised her hand to any of us. She never even raised her voice.

Grandma Rene was always put together. Even at home, she'd often have a dress on and always had her hair and makeup done. I remember I once made some offhand comment to Pops about how impressive it was that at her age she still had black hair. (She died in 1995 at the age of seventy-eight.) Pops looked at me like I had three heads and said in his dry, sardonic way, "She's been dyeing her hair for thirty years." I was like, *Grandma?!* I had no idea.

She didn't have a whole lot, materially—her house was a classic shotgun in a neighborhood that was as proud as it was poor—but she was appreciative of what she did have. She took care that the candy dish by the front door was always stocked—usually with peppermints, but sometimes you'd get lucky and there would be other flavors. She was a serious gardener, too, with a particular green thumb when it came to cucumbers (something my wife would replicate years later when she started a garden during the coronavirus pandemic). Grandma Rene also did well with corn. When I was young, I would go over and help get the garden ready, tilling the soil and dropping the seeds in.

We had a Sunday ritual where Mom would take us to her family's church every week, also in Cayce, and then we would have Sunday dinner at Grandma Rene's. My dad didn't go to my mom's church, or any church, but she took us by his mother's house every Sunday, which in my book makes her an exemplary daughter-in-law. She truly loved Grandma Rene.

Curtis Amaker, my biological grandfather, was long out of the picture. By the time I came along, Grandma Rene was married to a man we knew as Mr. Ed. That was his first name; I don't know what his last name was, but he was the man I knew as a grandfather figure, growing up. He'd had a pretty severe stroke, and he and Grandma Rene couldn't afford help, so she was his caretaker. He had lost the ability to talk and was confined to a wheelchair, and Grandma had to help put him to bed, get him out of bed, push him around, feed him, change him—she did everything for him. He clearly suffered a lot.

We had pretty much the same meal every Sunday: fried chicken, greens, rice and gravy, biscuits. Grandma Rene would make the biscuits from scratch. Sometimes she'd make cabbage, too. We would sit in the same seats around the table every week. It would be me, my mom, Ryan (my younger brother), Grandma, and Mr. Ed at the head of the table in his wheelchair. We'd all talk and Mr. Ed would stare at us.

The missing person in this scene is my father. He wouldn't go to church with us, and he wouldn't come to Sunday dinner at his mother's, either. He spent a lot of time at Grandma Rene's, just not on Sundays. He'd check in on her frequently during the week, on his way to the post office in the evening or coming back home in the morning. Once I was old enough, I would join him when he would load our lawn mower into our car and drive over to Cayce to cut her grass. I would help, and it became a bonding activity for Pops and me. I remember it fondly *now*. But at the time . . . the months between April and August in South Carolina can be unbearable during the day, especially right smack in the middle of the state, where we lived. So we'd be drenched in sweat, Pops and I, cutting Grandma's grass, he drinking his beer and smoking his cigarettes, me complaining. Thank God it was a power mower, not the manual push kind.

Pops really looked after Grandma Rene in a remarkably steadfast way. Even when he was at the height of his drinking, he always had time for her. I often saw him give her money, slipping a few bills in her hands. For her part, Grandma Rene always seemed to be able to get through to him; she was one of the few people he listened to. He had a special reverence and love for her, which was obvious, even to me as a kid. I think she was the one true emotional anchor in his life, more so than my mom or my brothers and me.

MY FATHER ALSO LOVED CAYCE, WHERE he grew up, and he always seemed to be happiest and most in his element there. He and I would sometimes walk from Grandma Rene's down to a laundromat that was run by a neighbor lady named Edith Washington who Pops was close to. She also sold snacks and candy and we would get Icees or pickles or sodas. There was invariably a jar of pigs' feet on the counter, but I stayed away from those. My mom later told me Mrs. Washington was like a second mother to Pops, looking out for him and trying her best to keep him on the straight and narrow.

Her laundromat was right next to what I'm going to call an auto repair shop, but that's an overstatement. My dad's buddies Bobby and Edward ran it as a sort of one-third repair shop and two-thirds social club. My dad drove a green 1973 Pontiac LeMans with an awful lot of miles on it—you're going to hear more about that car—so naturally there was always something that needed to be fixed or tinkered with. Pops would log serious hours down at Bobby and Edward's, just hanging out, drinking beer, solving the world's problems, and sometimes working on the car. Bobby and Edward were guys who he grew up with and who'd stayed in the neighborhood. As a kid, I really enjoyed the sense of fraternity in Cayce.

But Pops also used to hang out at a funkier place in Cayce that my mom called the Cut. It wasn't a club or bar; it was just a group of guys, typically ten or so, drinking beers in paper bags they bought at a small store around the corner, smoking cigarettes, and standing around outside in the back of someone's yard—it was literally a cut through behind a few houses. There was also gambling, some shooting of craps, but mainly there was a lot of loud talking. It was not a place for scripture reading or prayer.

Pops would go to the Cut for hours. And when he emerged from the Cut, you could tell where he'd been; he had what I came to think of as that Cut look—bleary eyes, wobbly walk, slurred speech. You could smell the alcohol on him; when someone drinks a six-pack or more on a hot day, it oozes out of their pores. Some of the earliest squabbles between my parents that I can remember involved his spending time back in the Cut. It was a place for grown men who wanted to get away from their wives and from the world. For Pops, it was like going to the neighborhood bar. I think it was his happy place.

The funny thing about the Cut is, it was only a block or so from the New Life Baptist Church, the place where we worshiped every Sunday. My dad, again, didn't go. But occasionally, when we were on the way to or from church, he would be at the Cut, so we could see him. Sometimes he'd wander out and say hi, and we'd continue on our way. The Cut definitely had a kind of mysterious attraction for me as a little boy; it was very much *not* a place where kids hung out. I did end up going back there a couple of times, when I was probably seven or eight. I remember feeling like I was a little older than I was, but also looking around and thinking, *I don't know what all the hubbub is about the Cut. This really isn't all that great. It's just a bunch of guys standing around drinking.*

Pops had a series of way stations, if you will, in Cayce. He would go to my grandma's house, the Cut, Bobby and Edward's, and Mrs. Washington's laundromat with the Icees and pigs' feet. Much of my father's life—and indeed all of our lives, when I was a child—revolved around Cayce, even though we lived across the river in Columbia, in a much nicer neighborhood. My mom told me that when she and Pops were looking at houses to buy in 1986, when I was seven—we were living in an apartment in Columbia when I was born—they had looked at a house or two in Cayce. But Mom made a conscious decision that Cayce would not be where Ryan and I grew up. She saw the often unhealthy hold that it had on Pops. Frankly, there wasn't a lot of good that came out of Cayce. It was where you went to kill time, where you went to drink. Grandma Rene's neighborhood was the poor part of town, segregated, literally the other side of the tracks. My dad and his buddies did not grow up with means, and that was pretty much the case for everyone else there we knew. There was a white section in Cayce, but we never saw it.

I've thought of what my life would have been like had we bought a place in Cayce, and I can guarantee things would have turned out very differently for me. I would have lived a far more segregated life, and like three of my cousins and other men I knew, I might have ended up enlisting in the military as a way of getting out. This is not a knock on the military, but my eyes likely would not have been opened by the schools in Cayce the way they were by the schools I was fortunate to attend in Columbia. I don't know that my mom and dad's marriage would have survived, either. Cayce never brought out the best in my father. Quite the opposite. Cayce was not generally a place where people thrived and were enabled to become their best selves.

It was a place where families stayed for generations, hampered by poverty and poor education, where people ended up marrying their neighbors because there weren't a lot of options to meet partners from other, larger social circles. There just weren't wide horizons in Cayce, for most people. It was a place where the Cut, as dispiriting as it was, served as an oasis from the disappointments in black men's lives. That was just the reality of Cayce; for so many people it was a dead end. Here's a true story that could also serve as a metaphor. A woman who lived a few doors down from Grandma Rene suffered from some form of mental illness, and every afternoon, for something like thirty-five or forty years, she would come out of her house and sweep the street. Basically, she was just moving the same dust back and forth.

What was interesting was that Pops had gotten out of Cayce and yet kept one foot back in. It felt like a world away from our neighborhood in Columbia, though it was only a short drive. Not that I don't have some fond memories of Cayce, but even as a child I thought, *This is not where I want to be ten years from now.*

MY MOTHER, BETTY JO WILEY, WAS born in Cayce, too, although when she was around ten years old, her family moved across the river to Columbia. Both my parents have lived their entire lives within a 20-to-25-mile radius of Cayce. Some years ago, in fact, I did a story on ancestry tracing with the Library of Congress. This was before DNA testing kits, when people would use birth records and death certificates to put together family histories. The Library of Congress's researchers found that in six generations my family had not left a fairly narrow slice of South Carolina. They were able to track the family back to the Charleston area, where we would have come in on slave ships, along with millions of other Africans. From there, we somehow made our way—or were taken—100 miles inland, to the Columbia area. The realities of those days aren't as long past as you might think. In fact my mom's mother grew up on a sharecropper's farm, picking cotton. Mom has memories of picking cotton, too, as a little girl while visiting relatives in the country.

So yes, my family has got *deep* South Carolina roots—even now. I live outside New York City, and I've got a second cousin on the South Side of Chicago, but otherwise pretty much all of our family is in South Carolina.

Aside from having been born in Cayce, my mom shared something else with my dad: an alcoholic father. His name was Franklin Delano Roosevelt Wiley. When he died in 1977, two years before I was born, he was already long gone from his family's life. He had been in and out of the Oliver Gospel Mission—a homeless shelter in downtown Columbia—and he essentially died alone, at the age of forty-four. Alcohol ruined his life, as my mother reminds me whenever she sees me after my second or third glass of bourbon or Cabernet. That was sort of a theme growing up, when we heard about Grandpa Frank, that drinking had crippled him—which would have been a tragedy under any circumstances, but he had a number of natural gifts. For one thing, he was wicked smart, an avid reader, and especially adept at math; he would help people in the neighborhood do their taxes despite having only briefly attended college. He was also, I've been told, quite the athlete—in particular a remarkable baseball player. There was also a certain mystery hovering over his background. He was adopted, and it was thought that one of his parents was white and one was black.

Frank's drinking had estranged him from much of the family by the time he died. He was an ugly drunk, and there are stories from that time that would make you cringe. He would go on a bender, beat my grandmother, disappear for a couple of days, and return—a cycle that went on for years.

I spoke to my mom for this book, too, exploring topics we'd never much discussed. Her memories of Grandpa Frank are hard ones. "If alcohol hadn't gotten in the way, there's no telling what he could have done," she told me. "But when he drank, he was a different person. He was crazy when he would drink." She said her dad had hit her a couple of times, too, "because I'm a fighter." She sometimes challenged him when he was going after her mom. That would bring repercussions. Once at the start of a school year, Mom was particularly proud of a brand-new *Dr. Kildare* notebook she'd bought—the old Richard Chamberlain series was one of her favorite TV shows. Frank, livid after she'd intervened in a fight, sought it out and ripped it up. For that little girl, her father's act was one of pure meanness. "That hurt me more than anything else he probably could have done," she said. Then she underscored something for me: "My daddy was abusive, but he wasn't a bad man. He was an alcoholic." He was pretty much out of the family's life by the time Mom was ten or eleven.

My grandmother was the one who kept the household together and did a remarkable job of rearing her four children. (Later, when she was in her sixties, she also adopted the son of one of her nieces who had died, raising him as well.) Her name was Florence Mildred Wiley. We called her Grandma Florence. She supported the family working for different school districts in the area as a custodian and a cafeteria lady—and earning extra money cleaning houses for white people. When she retired, she was at John P. Thomas Elementary School in Columbia, where my mom was a teacher. Some of my earliest memories are of going to see Grandma Florence in the evenings during the week, when she was at work. It would be my mom and me, sometimes Ryan, and we would just hang out with Grandma a little bit, talking, while she cleaned up classrooms, sweeping and mopping. That was her professional life. She hadn't gone to college, but she helped make sure that all four of her kids did. Education was very important to Grandma Florence.

When my mom was young, her grandfather, Grandpa Frank's father, helped care for her and her siblings, looking after them during the day and cooking meals while Grandma worked. Grandpa Frank's drinking had cost him a steady job working for a plastics company and whatever money he subsequently got his hands on he usually gambled away, so Mom's grandfather contributed some of his Social Security income, but the family was evicted from several homes. "Our stuff was actually put out on the street," Mom told me. A shotgun house they lived in for a period had holes in the floor.

The night before Mom's grandfather died, he gave Grandma Florence two hundred dollars; it was the money he owed on his own house in Cayce. "It makes me sad to have to think about," Mom said. "He told Mama, 'Go on, take this two hundred and pay off the house and you and the children will have a place to stay. Do not give the money to Frank. Do not tell Frank.' Well, the next day, what my mama did was give the money to my daddy, and he gambled it away." It was a huge loss and it still pains her. "Two hundred dollars was hard to come by. Twenty-five dollars was. None of us had that kind of money."

Not long after that, when Mom was in the fourth grade, the family's fortunes improved when Grandma met a man she became romantically involved with; she and Grandpa Frank never divorced, but like Grandma Rene, she and this new man would eventually have what was essentially a common-law marriage. He helped her buy a simple but solid brick house in Columbia, right off North Main Street. Back in the 1970s, it was an aspirational neighborhood. If you were black and you had a decent job, it was a neighborhood where you could buy a house.

When I was growing up, my mom would sometimes tell stories from when she was younger about having to borrow food from the neighbors. If Grandma Florence happened to be listening, she would bristle. She was proud of how far she had come and didn't always like to reflect on the harder periods of her life. She never really talked about my grandfather with us. Alcoholism and domestic abuse were not things you discussed back then.

Grandma Florence probably had the greatest influence on my life, outside of my mother. Her house was maybe ten minutes away from the apartment we lived in until 1986, and if I didn't see her every day, I certainly saw her every other day. She would often let me spend the night—a special treat—and in the morning she made great pancakes. I loved spending time with her. She had a slew of expressions that were applicable for just about any occasion. One of her favorites was "Ah, it's a time in the kingdom," which, translated, meant something like "That was some weird crap." If she saw a boy or a girl who was wearing a piece of clothing she thought was too tight or too small, she'd say, "Boy [or girl], who you stretching that for?" If we were at a family function and she felt like someone had eaten too much or heaped too much on his or her plate, she would say, "Girl [or boy], wish I had your appetite." When I think about these comments now, it occurs to me, *Wow, Grandma was kind of passive-aggressive, wasn't she?* But it didn't seem that way at the time. She was a flat-out riot.

Grandma Florence's more or less second husband was named Calvin Earl. We called him Mr. C.W. He was blind and wasn't very friendly—certainly not the sort of person who enjoyed small children. He died in 1989. But when I was growing up, he was always there in the house, not speaking to me or really anyone else for that matter, except Grandma.

Mr. C.W.'s blindness had been caused by diabetes. Like Grandma Rene with Mr. Ed, Grandma Florence spent a lot of time taking care of Mr. C.W., driving him places and shooting him up with insulin. That was a frequent topic of conversation at Grandma's: "Has Mr. C.W. had his insulin shot today? Someone has to give Mr. C.W. his shot." If Grandma was at work, her two youngest kids, Uncle Pop and Aunt Wanda, who lived with her, would have to do it. Sometimes my mom would take care of it. Giving Mr. C.W. his shot was a chore no one liked doing. I was glad I was a kid and it never fell to me.

Grandma Florence also had diabetes and had to give herself shots; the disease would eventually cost her both her legs. She tried to take care of herself, but even as a boy, I was aware she was eating things she shouldn't. Mom was constantly warning her, "Ma, you know you're not supposed to have that cake . . . Ma, you really shouldn't be eating that pie." Grandma Florence had a special fondness for cheesecake, and as I got older, I began to think, *Someday that cheesecake is going to kill her.* Unfortunately, I was more or less right.

Uncle Pop and Aunt Wanda were teenagers, much younger than my mom and her other sister, Aunt Ella, so they were fascinating to me—more like a big brother and sister than uncle and aunt. Pop is a nickname; his actual name is Franklin Delano Wiley, after his dad. He and Wanda would sleep in every Saturday morning, so if I had spent Friday night over there, I would get up and I could hang out with Grandma for a couple of hours, watch cartoons, eat the pancakes, then hang out with Pop and Wanda when they got up. They probably got tired of having me around, but they humored me. I enjoyed watching Pop play basketball in high school—he was good and got a scholarship to play in college. Wanda was a cheerleader at the games. She later drove me to middle school dances, and even taught me how to drive myself when I was finally old enough. She would become an important sounding board for me when I was a teenager.

The icing on the cake was that my cousin Cliff lived in a house right behind Grandma Florence's; his parents, Aunt Ella and Uncle Jake, shared a fence with Grandma. For much of my childhood, I could run over there, hop the fence, and play with Cliff or hang out with Grandma, Pop, Wanda—it felt like the perfect childhood, at least the Grandma Florence side of things.

BOTH OF MY GRANDMOTHERS WERE PILLARS of their churches. Mom's family had always worshiped at the New Life Baptist Church, where Grandma Florence sang alto in the Senior Musical Choir. In my quest to spend more time with her, I joined up, too. There were actually four choirs at New Life Baptist: the Jubilee Choir, for people north of sixty; the Senior Musical Choir, for middle-aged folks; the M. E. James Choir, for teenagers and young adults; and the Sunbeam Choir, for kids. I was the youngest member of my grandma's choir, a sort of mascot until I became old enough to sing and actually contribute. There wasn't a whole lot of variety in terms of hymns. The Jubilee Choir, for one, sang only eight or so different songs, which would rotate through the month. That was also the case at Mount Pleasant Baptist Church, where Grandma Rene worshiped. The services were pretty much interchangeable: same prayers, same hymns. At New Life Baptist, when it was time for the Jubilee Choir to sing, the pastor would instruct everyone to take out their hymnals and say something like, "All right, turn to number 484." As a kid, I thought that was hilarious. *They're singing the same songs month after month, year after year! At no point have these people committed them to memory?*

My favorite was "Guide Me, O Thou Great Jehovah," which came up in the rotation roughly every third Sunday. Every time the Jubilee Choir sang it, Sister Mabel McLendon, who sat in the first seat in the front row, would catch the Holy Ghost, which prompted her to gyrate and shout, with tears streaming down her face. In church, we called that "getting happy." Sister Mabel would get very happy.

It is hard to overstate how much time I spent in church growing up. Grandma Rene had a front porch, and after church, when I was five or six, I would walk back and forth on the porch and try and recite the sermon that I'd just heard. A lot of the family thought for sure I was headed for the ministry, but that path was something I never seriously considered, though I did stick it out long enough in the choir to become one of the lead singers and take a few solos. (Even now, when I'm home visiting, I'll occasionally run into an older person who knew one of my grandmas who will tell me, "I could have sworn you'd end up in the pulpit.")

Ryan and I still joke about the way our pastor, Reverend M.E. James, began every service with the same prayer. Even now, more than thirty years later, I remember how it started. "Oh Lord, our God, God of Abraham, God of Isaac, and the God of Jacob, the God of our forefathers who've gone on before us, holier is thy name than all the Earth. You have set the glories above the heavens." After that, it gets hazy. But Ryan and I would be in church chuckling when Reverend James would start his prayer. He led pretty much the same service every week for fifteen or twenty years.

It would be difficult to be as committed to the Lord as my grandmothers and my mother; you'd have to work really hard at it. My grandmothers in particular had had childhoods that were harder than most. Then they'd married and had children young, and adult life hadn't been much easier for either of them; one had been in prison, the other had survived abuse. Jesus Christ was not just a personal savior for them; he provided solace and hope—hope that life could be better. Beyond that, they loved the sense of community, particularly Grandma Rene, who had stopped working before I was born. When I knew her, Grandma Rene was only ever going to church, at church, or coming home from church.

Years ago, I heard a story told by a comedian whose name I can't recall that's always resonated with me. Growing up, he felt like his family spent nearly every single day at church. Monday, it was choir practice. Tuesday, the young people's meeting. Wednesday, the old people's meeting. Thursday, Bible study and potluck supper. Finally one Sunday, after the service had gone on for what felt like six or seven hours, he looked up at his grandma and said, "Grandma, just let me go to Hell. It can't be worse than this."

I often felt the same way, though looking back on it, I guess all the churchgoing worked. My brother and I both consider ourselves men of faith, although Ryan's faith would be sorely tested, along with our entire family's faith, during a tragic period several years ago, which I'll talk about in another chapter.

Pops did go to church one time, when I was nine or so, joining us at New Life Baptist Church. I remember it vividly because you just didn't see Dad sitting in a pew, aside from weddings and funerals. Reverend James even called him out at the end of the service, drawing the congregation's attention to my father's presence almost as if it were a miracle. Pops was so taken aback that I've often wondered if that's why he never went again.

From time to time he would make comments about, let's say, the hypocrisy of churchgoing people. He saw many of the folks who went to church on Sunday as fake and disingenuous. Some were men he'd see on other days in the Cut, drinking and gambling, men he also knew were womanizers. In his eyes, they were no holier than he was. Sometimes when he and my mother were having spats, he would even lump her in that category: someone who went to church on Sunday but didn't always practice the faith Monday through Saturday. When Reverend James called him out, I think his feeling was, *Yeah, I know what you all do the rest of the week. Don't call attention to the fact that I'm not usually here on Sunday and act like I'm lesser for it.*

Pops often has interesting, nontraditional takes on the news, and sometimes religion comes up in those contexts. For instance, I talked to him as I was leaving Minneapolis after covering the first funeral service for George Floyd, the black man who was killed by Minneapolis police in 2020, launching months of protest and renewed calls for racial justice. A number of religious leaders had spoken at the funeral, including the Reverend Al Sharpton. "What did you think of the service?" I asked Pops. He thought it was long—but then he pointed to the fact that even with so many ministers, pastors, and reverends speaking, not one had mentioned forgiveness. He acknowledged that perhaps the officers involved deserved to be punished, certainly prosecuted, but to have not one member of the Christian clergy mention forgiveness? That struck him as odd. He brought up the 2015 church shooting at Mother Emanuel AME in Charleston, when a white supremacist had killed nine African Americans at a Bible study class. The shooter was quickly arrested, and two days later, at a court hearing, a number of survivors and family members of victims said they forgave him. They didn't just forgive him; they forgave him almost overnight. Pops and I talked about the contrast with the George Floyd service. If he hadn't pointed it out, I probably wouldn't have thought about it.

That sort of conversation aside, Pops and I have never really spoken much about religion. I couldn't have told you what his core beliefs are, or if he even has Christian faith at all. I've seen him pray when it's called for, or when our whole family is bargaining with God, or maybe at a funeral, but I've never heard him utter the name of Jesus or talk about the Bible or redemption or Heaven and Hell. When I asked him point-blank what he believes, he replied, "I know there's a God. Everybody is going to have to give an account of their sins, or whatever, when Judgment Day comes."

"So you believe in that? You believe in the Bible and Jesus Christ?"

"Yeah."

"When you die, what do you think happens?"

"I think it's either you go into Heaven or you go into Hell, and it all depends on you having a relationship with God and asking him to forgive you and you taking charge of your life and becoming a better person."

He had clearly given the issue of religious hypocrisy some thought. "I had judgmental problems about churchgoing people where they can sneak and do whatever they want to do, do their little undercover dirty work, or whatnot, then thinking you're supposed to look up to them," he said. "Some of the people in church sound like Donald Trump: 'Don't do as I do. Do as I say to do.'"

He told me he'd gone to Mount Pleasant Baptist Church with Grandma Rene throughout his childhood, but that he pretty much quit once he left home. I asked why.

"I don't know. I guess I got on the wrong track." He said there was no particular reason he'd barely been back in the intervening fifty years: "I have no excuse." I told him I wasn't asking to be judgmental, just that I was curious if not going was a deliberate, conscious choice he'd made. He said no.

"Do you pray?" I asked.

"Yeah," he said.

"When?"

"You don't have to have no certain time to pray. You can walk around and pray."

I knew, I told him. "I just didn't know you were a prayerful person."

"Oh, I pray, man. I pray."

HERE'S SOMETHING ELSE ABOUT MY FAMILY I didn't know until I started writing this book: how my parents met, or what their court-ship was like, or why they finally decided to get married in 1982, three years after I came into the world and three and a half years before Ryan was born.

He and I had long been kind of mystified as to why they were together. They had certain things in common: being from Cayce, growing up with alcoholic fathers, being raised by more or less sin-gle mothers. Their families knew each other, Cayce being so small and incestuous. (When I was growing up, my two grandmas got on really well; Grandma Florence would sometimes join us for Sunday dinners at Grandma Rene's.) But beyond that, my parents didn't share a lot of interests. It wasn't just that Pops had little use for church. Mom, at that point in her life, was a teetotaler. Now she will occasionally have a glass of sweet wine with dinner if other people are having wine, but while I was growing up—never. I was well into my twenties before I saw her take even a sip of alcohol. Not only that, she didn't use profanity—not until Ryan and I were older and she ran out of words to get us to fall in line. (Ryan claims the first time he heard her curse was when he was in grade school. She blew up at me one morning when she found out I hadn't been walking him all the way to his bus stop the way I was supposed to: "How the Hell is he supposed to know where it is? He's only eight!" As Ryan told me recently, "I was so awed by the fact that Mom was cursing I couldn't even take delight in the fact that you were getting in trouble.")

Our mother was our father's opposite in every way, in terms of temperament and lifestyle. They didn't read the same books, and when I was growing up, I never saw them go out, just the two of them, to a movie or a restaurant. I've gotten the sense from people who knew them back in the day that Pops was something of a ladies' man—he had the big Afro and he drove the cool car—whereas my mom was meek and mild, shy, kind of a wallflower. Over time, that's changed: she's now the talker, a never-met-a-stranger type, while he's more reticent.

Pops graduated from high school in 1969. He was accepted at South Carolina State College (now University) but never enrolled. He told me: "I guess it was too soon to go to another school right off the bat for me." The war in Vietnam was at its height, and young men were still subject to the draft, but he enlisted in the Air Force on his own steam. "I kind of tried to better myself to get out of Cayce," he said. "I was just trying to find something that I thought I might like." He liked it enough to stay for four years, serving overseas at bases in Japan and Korea with a unit that helped pilots with all their flight gear—"hanging around a bunch of officers all day," as he described the assignment. He enjoyed the Air Force, "except them cold climates, Korea and Japan." Nevertheless, he left in February 1974 when Grandma Rene suffered some kind of health scare. He started at the downtown Columbia post office a month later.

He took on a new responsibility in 1977, when he fathered my half brother, Lawrence Meadows. He and Lawrence's mother didn't marry or live together, but he eventually started paying child support to Lawrence's maternal grandparents, who raised him. Thanks to the GI Bill, Pops had spent a year studying business administration at a technical school in Columbia while continuing to work, but his hours at the post office changed such that taking classes and studying became difficult, and he felt he had to make a choice. "Which would you rather do?" he asked me. "Go to school? Or go to work and get paid? It all depends on the individual, I guess. I ain't trying to be funny, but shoot, I was getting a check, so that schooling had to go." He said he liked his classes, but he didn't give me the impression he'd ever been a particularly committed student.

Meanwhile, as I mentioned, education was very important to my mother's family.

She was the oldest of her three siblings, and the first person in her family to graduate from college. She started at Johnson C. Smith University, a private HBCU (historically black college or university) in Charlotte, North Carolina, and then she transferred to Benedict College, another private HBCU, in Columbia, where she got a degree in elementary education. Mr. C.W. loaned Grandma Florence some of the tuition money; other relatives pitched in, too, and Mom worked odd jobs to support herself. In 1997 she would earn a master's in interdisciplinary studies from the University of South Carolina. But long before that, in 1978, when she was twenty-two, she got pregnant with me.

Pops told me Mom first caught his eye when she was still a teenager. He would go to watch her father pitch for the Cayce team in a local sandlot baseball league, and he saw her in the stands a couple times. They had a mutual friend who introduced them at some point, and Pops said he would occasionally talk to Mom and her sister Ella when he'd run into them. It wasn't until several years later, when he was stationed at the Shaw Air Force Base not far from Columbia, that they re-met at a party and actually started dating.

Mom was sixteen then, a junior in high school, and it took a year or two for the romance to kindle. "Your dad was fly-by-night," she told me recently. "I mean he got my phone number, whatever, but maybe he called once. I called him a couple times and he didn't call back. We didn't have cell phones then. We had house phones"—meaning if Pops did call, he might not have gotten through the checkpoint of Grandma Florence. "Mama never really liked your dad. She thought he was too old, and I think he reminded her of Daddy."

Pops knew Grandpa Frank, who he sometimes ran into in Cayce, but he didn't have much to do with him. "He was like my daddy. He was a wino. Me and him would talk and he said, 'I know you like my daughter, but no matter what you do or what she do, I don't want you putting your hands on her.'" In other words, Grandpa Frank, who used to hit Grandma Florence, was telling my dad not to do the same. "That was about it," Pops said of conversations with his future father-in-law.

In Mom's account, she and Pops were a pretty serious couple her freshman year in college—they actually got engaged—but after a while the relationship cooled and became more of an on and off thing. The period when Pops fathered my half brother, Lawrence? "That was off," she said.

Dare I say it's become slightly more socially acceptable to have a child out of wedlock? But back then, as you might imagine, my own impending arrival did not sit all that well with Grandma Florence. Her innate dislike of my father had been compounded by the fact that Pops already had a son; there was, shall we say, a reluctance to accept him with open arms. All the same, Mom said he was support-ive during her pregnancy and that he went with her to the hospital for my birth, though he wasn't in the delivery room the way fathers are now.

Mom had been living with her aunt Marg (short for Margaret), but they had a falling-out, and there wasn't room for Mom and me at Grandma Florence's, so Pops got an apartment and they moved in together. It wasn't particularly romantic, though—even by the low romantic standards of a couple with a squalling newborn. "We were living together, but your dad still had his life and his friends," Mom said. "I remember once some girl called. Someone else he was seeing sent a gift for you. There was more or less an understanding that we lived together but we didn't really *live* together, if that makes sense. I needed a place and we got along good."

Nevertheless, my pending birth represented a scandal for many in the community. Mom was actually shunned by the Reverend James, who forced her to get up in front of the entire New Life Baptist Church congregation one Sunday and apologize, beg for forgiveness. He then prayed for her, and for me, still in her womb, asking God that I be born a "blessed child" even out of wedlock. Four decades later, she and I chuckle about the fact that a lot of those same people who were so quick to judge her about her bastard son back in the late 1970s will happily make it known today that they proudly watch her son on TV and will sometimes even ask for favors involving that son.

Here's something even more ironic: Reverend James, who was married, is believed to have carried on an affair with a close female relative of ours for years. My mom even found a photo of him in one of the relative's jewelry boxes after she died.

I'm sure my mom's experiences at the New Life Baptist Church influenced my dad's feelings about churchgoing and Christian forgiveness. At any rate, the congregation must have accepted her apology, as Mom was a faithful congregant for another two decades (until our family started attending a new church in West Columbia). I was surprised when Pops told me that he and Mom hadn't been married at New Life Baptist. In his telling, "We were downtown or something, and she wanted to get married and I was kind of scared to get married. And I said, 'Well, we'll go up here to this courthouse and see if it's open,' and it was, and we just got married. It was on an impulse or a spur of the moment or whatever you want to call it. We just up and got married."

Like always, my mom offers a more nuanced narrative. She had reached a breaking point, she told me. "We had to do something because I couldn't keep living like that. You started asking questions because your last name was Wiley—my name." Push came to shove when she gave my dad an ultimatum: "Either we get married or Craig and I have to go home." She said Pops hated the idea of another man potentially raising me, so he finally put a ring on it.

The date was September 2, 1982. I was three. There was a subsequent reception that I've seen pictures of—there's a cute one of me in a small dark suit, hovering near a punch bowl, a surefire attraction for a three-year-old—but I have no memories of any of it.

IT WAS PROBABLY NOT TOO LONG after that when I met my dad's father for the first and only time. Curtis Amaker had been living for years in Swansea, a small town of several hundred people outside of Columbia, where his family apparently owned a house and some land. Pops told me he would drive over to Swansea to visit his father "every once in a while." That surprised me, given everything else Pops had told me about their relationship, or lack thereof. I asked what they would do together on those visits.

"We would talk for a little while, or this or that. I didn't stay long.

I just went to see how he was doing, or whether he was still living or whatnot."

"Why did you feel the need to go check on him?"

"I guess it wasn't my fault that he was my dad. So I guess it had something to do with somebody being your daddy, and, you know, you just want to check on him and see how he's doing."

Eventually a sister of Curtis's who lived in New York sold the family's property and moved him to the Bronx, where he died in 1985. The sister then had his body sent back down to South Carolina for my father, his only child, to deal with. As Pops explained it to me, "Somebody asked me one time, 'What's the most money you ever wasted?' And I told him, 'The two thousand and something dollars I paid for my daddy's funeral.'"

That surprised me, too. "You paid for a funeral of a man you didn't even know?"

"Well, I knew him, but I paid for a funeral of a man that never did do anything for me. I'll put it that way."

CHAPTER 2

DAD AND MOM AND ME

Pops never drank hard liquor. He was strictly a beer guy. For decades, he drank only Budweiser, then at some point switched over to Coors Light. Later, when things got bad, he drank whatever beer he could get his hands on, whatever was cheapest. Cigarettes were his other constant. He invariably had a Newport in one hand, a beer in the other—in the house, in his bed, in the yard, at Bobby and Edward's, cutting Grandma Rene's grass.

And behind the wheel of his 1973 Pontiac LeMans. It was painted an intense metallic emerald hue that you could see coming from blocks away and that Pontiac labeled "verdant green." It had an all-white interior and a matching white vinyl top, which Pops was particularly proud of. Inevitably, when he was driving there would be a couple of eight-track tapes on the passenger seat floor, old-school R&B or funk that he would listen to from time to time. There would also be a Budweiser in a plastic cup, stuck in a small gap between the front seats, and hanging out of his mouth, a cancer stick. The windows would be down, not because of the smoke but because the car's air conditioner never worked properly. Long before everyone acknowledged that doing so was terribly dangerous, Pops was literally drinking and driving—and without either of us or anyone else in the car wearing seat belts. As I look back on it now, I wonder, *What the hell was he thinking? What was my mom thinking letting us ride with him?* He received several DUIs over the years, and he caused a couple of relatively minor accidents—including one that helped us finally get him into rehab—but fortunately he was alone on all those occasions.

A host of reasons kept him from being the dad I wanted him to be—the dad I needed. He didn't set out to be a bad father, he didn't *want* to not be around, but in a way, he became a parent with both hands tied behind his back, hindered by his family history, his own parents' shortcomings and dearth of resources, his lack of a good role model in his own father. There was the systemic and overt racism he faced as a black man of his generation. And there was the legacy of alcoholism—and likely an undiagnosed underlying depression. Was his drinking in part an attempt to self-medicate? Possibly. My dad spent the better part of his life unhappy about various aspects of his life, and he found comfort and solace in alcohol. For most of his life he was able to manage it to a certain extent—until he couldn't.

Back in the day, however, when I was very little, I thought he was the epitome of cool. He was a 1970s guy through and through—almost like he'd been frozen in time when Jimmy Carter was in office. The aging LeMans and the eight-tracks on the floor were only part of it. He kept his hair in an Afro through most of my childhood, and well into the nineties he would wear shirts with butterfly collars and pants made from an array of polyesters. It was ages before I ever saw Pops in a simple pair of jeans.

My dad's refusal to chase trends was kind of admirable. He had a timeless sense of style, let's say. One thing I genuinely admire about him is that he's comfortable in his own skin. To put it bluntly, he doesn't give a shit what other people think about him. But by the time I entered middle school, like most kids that age, I had grown very self-conscious about him. I thought, *What the heck, Pops. You are a public embarrassment.* It wasn't just the drinking; he was also such a throwback. He still is. He didn't have a cell phone until 2018, and he still refuses to text. He doesn't have an email account, either; in fact I've never seen him use a computer.

It's all a reflection of his personality: he's stubborn and, his former vices aside, careful with his money. Pops hasn't made a car payment my entire life, not since the Ford administration. He bought the LeMans new, in 1972, while he was in the Air Force. After it finally died in the 2000s, he drove hand-me-down cars: first a white Buick LeSabre from his sister Carrie Mae; then a Mercury Topaz from his brother James (which became my first car); and then Grandma Florence's 1993 Honda Civic. For a while, he was even driving a 1980s vintage wheelchair-accessible van that Mom had bought to transport Grandma Florence when she was near the end of her life.

To this day, Pops doesn't have a debit or credit card. He used to say, "If you can't buy something in cash, minus a house or a car, then you don't really need it." He lived that. On Fridays, growing up, if we needed cash for something over the weekend, like going out or shopping, we'd have to put in a request Thursday night or, at the latest, early Friday morning. He would go to the bank on Friday, and that would be it for the weekend—a real pain when I became a teenager.

His range of interests is very narrow. He never developed hobbies or passions other than drinking and smoking, and for most of his life he didn't hang out with people who didn't do one or both. There was a period, when I was very young, where he was active in a softball league, but he told me he and his friends drifted away when there was a move to make the league co-ed. He then joined a bowling league, where he was on a team from the post office. Friday nights, my mom would drop me off at the Brunswick Bowling Lanes on Bush River Road to root him on. I liked seeing Pops with friends from his job; getting to hang out with them made me feel cool. Pops was a pretty solid bowler, though it was clear that the evenings were as much about camaraderie, smoking, and drinking as about bowling strikes. I would watch for a bit, but eventually he would give me a little money and I'd go off to play video games or eat bowling alley hot dogs. Over the years, though, participation in the league started dwindling, and Pops, along with most of his colleagues, gave the sport up.

I suppose you could argue that his constant tinkering with the LeMans was a hobby. It broke down so often I couldn't begin to count the hours and days I spent with him under the hood, and sometimes under the car itself. He was always working on it, with me as his designated assistant. He had a Chilton repair manual for old Pontiacs that was eight hundred pages thick, practically an encyclopedia. Whenever I saw him thumbing through it, I knew I was about to be drafted into helping him on a project that could take anywhere from two days to two weeks to what felt like a decade—never just a couple of hours. He would work on the LeMans mornings, when he got home from the post office. He'd work on it late at night, on weekends, whenever.

This is not an exaggeration: there was always something wrong with that car. I sat second chair on three or four carburetor changes and countless other operations and interventions. On one occasion Pops dragged me to a junkyard out in rural South Carolina, where we traipsed around looking for some obscure part for a car that at that point was approaching twenty years old. I couldn't have been more than eight or nine. *Damn, Pops, what are we doing out here?* I thought. *I know we're not rich, but we can afford a used car. We don't have to live like this.* I lost count of the number of times he had to get the LeMans towed or Mom and I would have to go pick him up somewhere after it had broken down. Pops and I have joked about how much money he put into it—two or three new cars' worth. But for a large swath of my childhood and youth, his beloved verdant green LeMans was the bane of my existence.

Imagine you're a kid. It's a Saturday morning, and you want to play with friends or watch cartoons, but your dad says, "Hey, can you come out and help me with the car?" *Ah, dang it. Again with the LeMans?* I might have been more enthusiastic if he had been teaching me something or letting me get my hands dirty, but he didn't trust me to work on the car and that never changed. I never got promoted. By that I mean, at six years old I'm handing him a socket wrench and holding a flashlight, and at fifteen I'm still doing the same thing. As I got older, I realized it wasn't about my actually being useful in any serious way. It wasn't about my contributing. It was just about my being there. He wanted a buddy.

That didn't mean he necessarily wanted to talk, however. One thing about my dad is that he's comfortable in silence. He's not one of those people who have to talk to fill a void. Over the years, I've been told, "You're a good interviewer because you listen. You'll let someone just talk and not interrupt them." And I think that's something I got from Pops. Underneath the hood of the LeMans, we could go ten, fifteen, twenty minutes without saying a thing, aside from his cussing at the car. We were just together, being in the moment. That was our hang. I didn't have a choice in the matter, but as I grew older, I learned to tolerate and even appreciate it.

I suspect working on the LeMans together was a way for a man who had a hard time connecting with people to be available for me, to be a father. From time to time he would try to impart certain life lessons. He used to say, "Keep your nose clean." That was one of his favorite sayings. Or "Don't go taking any wooden nickels"—whatever that actually means. Even his advice was old-school, though another favorite, "Don't go doing drugs," was more up-to-date. These life lessons would usually come while we were under the hood of the LeMans. When I got a little older, he added, "Don't go getting a girl pregnant," to the menu. That was as close as we ever got to him giving me a talk about the birds and the bees. He must have assumed I picked up the rest of it in school or at least the schoolyard, which was a correct assumption.

Like a lot of fathers and sons, we had one fail-safe subject we could always talk about and bond over: sports. One of my favorite memories of spending time with him was when I was nine and he took me to a preseason NFL game in Columbia—just him and me. The "home" team was the Washington Redskins, as the team was then known, and there was a quarterback under center named Doug Williams who looked a lot like us, which is how I became a lifelong Washington fan.

Aside from under the hood of the LeMans, the other place I tended to have conversations with Pops was in his and Mom's bedroom. They shared it, but the bedroom always felt like his territory. Between his drinking and his working the third shift at the post office, he was in bed a lot during the afternoons, and since Mom was still at work, he was the parent in charge by default. Sometimes he would be watching the TV set they had on a dresser, but more often I would have to wake him up if I needed his permission to go outside and play with a friend or go up the street to someone's house. Oftentimes he wouldn't remember that he'd given me permission, because he had then passed out from drinking or had been in a deep sleep from which I'd roused him. This gave me the advantage of plausible deniability on those occasions when I hadn't actually bothered to ask permission.

I don't mean to suggest that I didn't take him seriously as an authority figure. Not at all. There was an incident when I was in middle school and stumbled upon the joys and wonders of pay-per-view porn. I thought—if you can call this thinking—*Oh, great! I'll order one or two pornos, and no one will ever know.* Well, a few weeks later the itemized cable bill turned up and Mom was aghast, so much so that she decided to haul out the big gun, which was Pops. She used him only for the direst transgressions.

He was in the bedroom, of course. She marched me back there, waving the bill. "Your son and these movies! You've got to talk to him about it!" My dad's response was almost hilariously succinct: "You're way too young for that. Cut it out." It wasn't funny in the moment, though. I was scared. Pops didn't get bogged down in the daily minutiae of parenting, so when he did chime in, even when Mom had forced him to, you knew you had messed up big-time. Believe me, I stopped ordering porn.

POPS HAD STARTED AT THE POST office as a manual clerk, hand-sorting pieces of mail that for whatever reasons were rejected by the automated letter-sorting machine (LSM). Then he was promoted to working one of the LSMs. There were a couple of times, early in his career, where he was up for further promotions, but he took himself out of the running. "I'd been offered to do management," he told me, "but I never did take it."

"Who turns down management?" I asked.

"Anybody that don't want the headaches, or the responsibilities of other people not working or not doing what they're supposed to do or whatnot."

"Would it have been more money?"

"Yeah, it would have been a little more, but I didn't think it was worth it. 'Hey, Melvin, you want to get in the supervisors program, became a supervisor?' '*Nope.*'"

He told me he didn't even take a moment to think it over. All the same, his work ethic was unbeatable. For one thing, he chose to work the brutal third shift since it paid better, and he often added extra shifts and worked holidays, for the overtime. His reliability, which he was proud of, was especially impressive given how much he was drinking. There were times when he'd drink all day and pass out, but he'd still get up for that third shift. For years, he did that. No matter how lousy he felt—and I'm sure he felt lousy *a lot*—he never took a sick day and barely ever a vacation. A couple of times his bosses made him take a week off. "You've *got* to take some days," they told him. "You can't just hoard vacation time." When he retired, he had months of it built up.

That discipline carried over to the other formal responsibilities in his life. He was scrupulous about paying child support every month for Lawrence, my older half brother who lived with his grandparents, ninety miles away from us. Not only that: Pops continued his payments even after Lawrence had turned eighteen, when he legally could have stopped. Just because he thought it was the right thing to do, he kept sending checks to Lawrence's grandmother until she died, long after Lawrence had attended college and graduated.

At home Pops left most of the day-to-day child-rearing and household chores to Mom; he was often checked out on those fronts. But in a crisis he would step up in a big way. There was the time when I was seven and Ryan was barely a toddler when my mom had to have surgery. It was nothing life-threatening, but she was in the hospital for almost a week, and out of commission for another week when she got home. Pops actually took the time off from work; he was suddenly the parent bathing us, feeding us, dropping me off and picking me up from school. At the time, it all seemed very weird—that's how unusual Pops being hands-on was, though he would cook on occasion. He had three go-to "dad cuisine" dishes: beef stew, pigs' feet, and what we called "meaty rice," which was pieces of chicken boiled with rice, onions, and celery. There may have also been some takeout employed while Mom was in the hospital.

I wouldn't say Pops was especially pleased with his career, but he enjoyed the fellowship at the post office and he appreciated the security and the government benefits, including the pension he now receives. For his generation especially, civil service was a rung on the ladder to the middle class. If you didn't go to college, if you didn't have a degree, working in a place like the post office or getting a job with the state or landing some other public sector work was your best chance at providing a decent standard of living for your family, which my dad did. We didn't have a ton of money growing up, but we didn't really want for much.

Aside from the hours, the biggest issue Pops had with his job was the monotony; he was basically an assembly-line worker for the better part of four decades. Some things about it were interesting to him. He would talk occasionally about all the different magazines to which people subscribed. He would sometimes even read them before sorting them. He knew all of the zip codes in the area by heart, so we had a game in which you could give him any local address and he would rattle off its zip code. That always tickled me.

When I was little, he worked at the main post office branch in downtown Columbia. (As the postal service shrank, he was eventually moved to a processing facility in the town of Dixiana, twenty miles away.) I went to visit a few times in the mornings before his shift ended, while I was pretty little. I was awestruck by the operation itself—all the machines, the scale and complexity of it. Pops wore a blue denim apron with *American Postal Workers Union* on the front, which kept his clothes clean, and he had thimble-like rubber caps that he wore over his thumbs to help sort the mail. For a kid, it was all really cool.

As time went on, more and more of his work became automated. He would talk about that—how it made his job easier but also more boring. He once brought up the phrase "going postal," and said, "If you've ever worked at the post office, you know how real a possibility that is." He was joking, to a point. I recently asked him if he regretted retiring relatively early, at the age of sixty-three, in 2013, after thirty-nine years on the job. He laughed. "Thirty-nine years and somebody's going to regret that?"

MY MOM STARTED HER CAREER AS a preschool teacher, but the pay was horrible and she ended up working at a bank, Security Federal, as a teller and retirement advisor. Visiting her on the job was less exciting than going to the post office, but I was impressed when I saw her behind a desk in such a serious, quiet, important-looking place. I also liked the green lollipops the bank used to give out.

Education was where Mom's heart lay, though. In 1986, when I was seven, she started teaching kindergarten at Kelly Miller Elementary School, in Winnsboro, South Carolina. It was a forty-five-minute commute each way, and that's how I became a latchkey kid. She would have to leave early, before I was off to school, and she would get home long after I did. Ryan would be at an informal day care setup at a neighbor's house, and Pops would be home, but asleep or drunk or both.

Once she started teaching, part of my summer ritual became

helping Mom set up her classroom for the new school year. It was fun when I was younger, but less so as I got older and came to resent having my summer interrupted by tasks like decorating walls and stapling things to bulletin boards. School was the last place I wanted to be during summer vacation. Maybe it was Mom's version of Pops's making me work on the LeMans or help him cut Grandma Rene's lawn.

There were certain other drawbacks to having a mom who was a teacher. She was adamant about making sure that Ryan and I were involved in a slew of extracurricular activities, some of which we enjoyed, but some we did not. She had me playing soccer in elementary school for a guy named—I kid you not—Coach Rambo. On Saturday mornings, for a brief period, I took magic classes—that was more my thing, but she supported it. More her thing was my playing the violin for several years in the school orchestra before switching to the string bass for another year or two. My musical education started in fifth grade, and I didn't enjoy either instrument. My fingers were too fat for the strings. I never practiced. I wasn't particularly good. But she thought it was important to expose me to classical music. I understand this now. But back then I didn't want to be there, and my patient teacher, Mr. Preston, knew I didn't want to be there. I felt foolish. Pops at some point even complained about the cost of renting the violin from a music store. It was all part of Mom's master plan to keep us so busy we wouldn't have time to get into trouble.

This continued through middle school and high school. I was in student government. I was captain of the debate and Model UN teams. As Cadet Lieutenant Colonel Craig Melvin, I became the group commander of my high school's Air Force Junior ROTC. I competed in oratorical contests organized by the American Legion, the Elks, and the Optimist Club. I ended up winning a fair amount of scholarship money, $10,000, although that was likely a result of my having little to no competition. Not a lot of kids were clamoring to orate, then or probably now, but my mom . . . Well, I was going to write "forced me into it," but that's too strong, even if it sometimes felt that way. Let's just say my mom "encouraged" these sorts of activities.

Needless to say, I wasn't one of the cooler kids at school. I wore Coke-bottle glasses from the time I was four or five—I didn't discover contact lenses until I was in college—and up until middle school Mom would dress me in nerd clothes: lots of plaid shirts under sweaters, Dockers khakis, white leather shoes. Worse, every Sunday she had me iron all my clothes for the coming week. This was the early nineties, when Steve Urkel, the super nerd played by Jaleel White, was the breakout character on the sitcom *Family Matters,* so yeah, my friends liked to invoke that comparison. At home I was like someone living in a totalitarian state; I didn't realize there were kids in other families who had a modicum of freedom when it came to getting dressed every day

In middle school, I was allowed to make some of my own fashion choices. I was finally able to wear T-shirts and jeans on occasion. I think the first T-shirt I ever wore to school had Bo Jackson on it, but I wouldn't say my taste was impeccable. I wore my hair in a Gumby for a while—that was about the most rebellious I ever got hair-wise—and later a high-top fade. There was a two-year period where I wore extremely garish Cross Colours jeans, but once I retired those in high school, that was the end of my chasing trends and trying to be cool. The sad thing was, I kept ironing all my clothes every Sunday all through high school. It wasn't until I got to college that I realized *not* ironing was even an option in life.

My peers eventually decided it would be socially acceptable to be seen with me, but I wouldn't say I had the most robust teenage social life. On Friday nights, even in high school, I didn't go to the football games. I never hung out. I didn't go to parties. All the extracurricular activities kept me busy, but Mom also had me on a really tight leash. She knew all my friends. She had relationships with all my friends' parents. Even when I was in college, she made a point of knowing my friends, not least when I joined a fraternity (and maybe *especially* then). There just wasn't much room to fall out of line in the Melvin household. She held Ryan and me accountable. Once when I was in elementary school, she spanked me for bringing home a report card that wasn't abysmal but didn't represent my best work. Spanking was part of my upbringing, just not usually for report cards, and she finally stopped mid-swat and said, "What am I doing?" Even for her, this was a little much.

More typical of her style of discipline was an occasion when I was nine or ten. We were at a church function and the Sunday school teacher, who was ancient—she'd been at New Life Baptist since Moses led the Israelites out of Egypt—asked me to render the Lord's Prayer in front of everyone. I swear, I must have heard the Lord's Prayer several thousand times by that point in my life, but I didn't know it from beginning to end and I stumbled reciting it, which embarrassed my mother to no end. In her eyes, I had brought shame upon the family, and in church, no less. That would be the last time I was unable to recite the complete Lord's Prayer. At home that night, Mom forced me to practice it for a few hours, and for a few more hours the next morning. You did not embarrass the family, and you did not embarrass my mother. If you did, you did it once, and it was a long time before you did it again.

IN 1986, WHEN I WAS SEVEN, the same year my mom started teaching, we moved from our apartment to a house in a middle-class development in Columbia called Pine Valley. We had driven around and looked at different places, with me wowed by the idea of living in a house as opposed to the two-bedroom, one-bath apartment I'd known my entire life. When we bought a house that not only had three bedrooms and two baths, but a garage and a backyard, I thought we'd really come up in the world. A big selling point for my mom was the fact that Pine Valley was in a solid school district.

There was another selling point for Mom, which I only recently learned. "One stipulation I always had," she said, "was that it had to be a house I could make the house payments on if your daddy left. I had to be able to afford it on my own because I saw what my mama went through."

The area has changed—it's now 70 percent African American—but back in the 1980s and 90s, before white flight, Pine Valley was incredibly diverse. We lived on Chandler Avenue. The folks across the street, a woman and her son, were white. Next door to them, there was a black woman and her son. On the corner were the Najims, who were Lebanese and owned a hair salon and some other businesses. They had a son, Daniel, who was about two years younger than me and a friend. His older sister, Nancy, was my first neighborhood crush.

Across the street from the Najims, back on our side of the street, were the Fungs, who owned a nearby Chinese restaurant. They were an immigrant family; the parents spoke little to no English and had to rely on their daughter, Lily, to translate. Next to the Fungs was the Pendarvis family, who were black. And next door to us on one side was a white family, the Bryants, and on the other side a black family, the Roundtrees, who had two girls and a boy, Brian, who was Ryan's age. They were buddies from preschool: Ryan-and-Brian.

If you saw a neighborhood as diverse as ours on a TV show, you'd almost think the producers were trying too hard to check every box.

All in all, it was a pretty solid place to grow up, with lots of space and a ton of kids. We played basketball and baseball in our backyard. The Najims had a pool. We were constantly in and out of one another's houses. In that sense, it was a classic 1980s suburban childhood, like out of *Stranger Things* or an old Steven Spielberg movie. All the houses in Pine Valley were built in the late 1970s and early 1980s, from four or five basic designs, so if you went over to a friend's, you more or less already knew the layout. Like most of them, ours was vaguely ranch style, one story, part brick, part wood, and painted tan with dark brown shutters.

The mix of families helped shape and mold me in ways that I didn't fully appreciate until later in life. When you grow up interacting with different kinds of people, you find it a lot easier as an adult interacting with different kinds of people—and that, of course, is a huge part of being a journalist. Ryan and I both regret that the neighborhood is now much less diverse. "It was extremely sad to see folks start to pick up and leave for 'better communities,'" he recently wrote me. That was a process that began when he was still in school, and all the families I've mentioned have long since moved. In fact, there are only two families from my childhood still living on Chandler Avenue: the Roundtrees and mine.

Vince Roundtree and Pops had an interesting relationship. Mr. Vince, as we called him, was an applications engineer and Pops's polar opposite in many ways: he was a devout churchgoer, and as far as I know he never drank, smoked, swore, or even raised his voice. He was quiet and mild-mannered—but he also drove an old red Volkswagen Beetle that made so much noise you always knew, whether you wanted to or not, when he was leaving for work or coming home. Mr. Vince was a front-yard mechanic, like Pops, constantly tinkering with that VW, so they bonded over their shared ability (or frequent lack thereof) to get their borderline antiques moving again. Mr. Vince's garage was almost like an auto shop, he had so much gear and equipment, and there was a constant traffic in borrowed tools between our two houses.

One other important house on the street belonged to the Viscontis, Joe and Nonna, who didn't have kids. They were Italian, and Joe, though he was fifteen years older than Pops, was one of my dad's only genuine friends. They had a special bond because Joe had also worked at the post office and he also drove a 1973 LeMans—a brown one, though, and without a vinyl top like ours, which Pops liked to point out to Joe. I would often hang out with the two of them in Joe's garage, where he had a mini-fridge usually stocked with beer. Joe would drink one; Pops would drink three or four. They would talk cars, sports, and politics, my dad occasionally getting a little loud when he'd had too many. They'd argue sometimes, but only in fun. When I was older and home from college, I would sometimes share a beer or two with them—I have to admit, being able to drink at Joe's house made me feel like a grown man. But the key thing to know about the Viscontis was they were religious about watching *The Price Is Right*. You could not interrupt. If Pops went over there while *The Price Is Right* was on, he'd have to wait until the show was over for Joe to head out to the garage.

I had a memorable conversation with Joe and Pops when I was in my twenties and had recently been named the main evening news anchor at WIS-TV, the NBC affiliate in Columbia. It came up that my parents had paid a little over $60,000 for our house in 1986. That was less than my new annual salary. The disparity struck me. I realized they must have struggled financially more than I had fully appreciated. It couldn't have been easy to raise two kids, support another, and cover a mortgage on the combined salaries of a postal worker and a public school teacher. Not that we ever talked about money growing up (along with all the other things we didn't talk about), but buying that house was a big accomplishment for them.

MY EXPERIENCE GROWING UP IN A diverse neighborhood was profoundly different from my parents' childhoods. My mom is old enough to remember Klansmen driving through Cayce to intimidate people, and the fear of having a cross burned on her lawn. She remembers having to enter the front of a bus, pay her fare, then exit and board through the rear door to get to the black seats in the back. She was nine when the Civil Rights Act passed in 1964, but even then, she told me recently, "If you sat on the bus by someone who was white, they got up and moved." That continued into her teenage years.

She found the climate better in Columbia, after the family moved, but there were still issues. From time to time Mom would tell Ryan and me stories about riding on the school bus with other black students and having rocks thrown at them. There was an incident where someone spat at her. She was part of the first class to integrate her high school, A. C. Flora High School. That was in the fall of 1970, when she was a freshman, sixteen years after *Brown v. Board of Education*. A. C. Flora had been almost 100 percent white, and one way the school's administration responded to an influx of black students was by suspending or expelling upwards of half of the five hundred new students. That was so outrageous it even made *The New York Times*, which quoted the principal disdaining the new students as "poorly dressed" and "uncouth" and blaming the suspensions and expulsions on "a cultural and class thing, not racial." *Sure.* Years ago when I was at MSNBC, I had a guest on who is an important figure in the South Carolina Republican Party. He's a friendly guy whom I've had a good working relationship with as a reporter. He was also a big wheel in student government at A. C. Flora when Mom was there, and she does not recall the same friendly politico whom I've come to know, though the racial divide in her high school was more nuanced than you might think: a few black kids, those whose parents were professionals, were accepted by the white kids, while kids with poorer backgrounds like Mom's were shunned. She was the school's first black student body treasurer, by the way.

I have to say those kinds of stories sounded foreign to Ryan and me growing up. We had read about the civil rights era, but it seemed distant from our lives, at least until Mom discussed her experiences. For his part, Pops almost never talked about how being black affected him as a boy. I had thought he had attended segregated schools his entire childhood, but here's yet another thing I learned after interviewing him: in the fall of 1968, at the start of his senior year, he, too, was among a first group of black students at Brookland-Cayce High School, which was formed by combining a black school and a white one.

"Was everyone friendly?" I asked

"You think about it," Pops said. "No, no, no."

He told me he never heard anyone use the N-word, but hostility was expressed all the same. "It was the way they looked at you," he said. "When you were walking down the hall, you had to walk on a certain side, and whatnot. You ain't talking to somebody who went to school in New York. This was the South. The white teachers didn't want you in class in the beginning." He said he had to walk to Brookland-Cayce every morning, a mile and a half away: the school buses didn't serve the black side of town, even in winter, when it can get cold and wet. "You put on your coat and put on your hat and put on your boots and keep moving." Since he already had most of the credits he needed to graduate, he was lucky in that he needed to take only a couple of courses anyway. He worked in the afternoons and evenings washing dishes at a Howard Johnson's, which took up most of his time and energy. "I said, 'Shoot, what else am I going to do? Them people don't want me in their class, so I don't want to go.' So I just didn't."

Amazingly, Pops told me that before senior year he had had almost no contact with white people whatsoever: "It was just the black schools and the white schools. And the white folks lived in a certain place and they stayed on their side of the track, and we stayed on our side, I guess."

That sounds like such a different world than the one I grew up in, at least on the surface. Mom likes to say she raised Ryan and me to be color-blind, and to some extent that is true. Thanks to her and to the diverse neighborhood we grew up in, we assimilated pretty well. I had friends of all races and was able to move between different groups in middle school and high school easily. We had our table in high school where we all sat, my closest friends and I. But I'd also go sit at the football table or the white kids' table. Sometimes I'd hang out with the art kids, who really didn't fit in anywhere. I even befriended the band geeks. I bounced around between all these cliques. I've always been gregarious and there just wasn't a group with whom I couldn't get along.

That said, I wasn't oblivious to the social implications of race. I got used to being the one black kid getting up to speak at Model UN or debate club, the one black kid at an oratorical contest, the one black kid at a Key Club function. I was aware of that, but I was never consumed by it. There were times when I caught flack for allegedly "acting white." There was an African American kid in high school, a football player, who nicknamed me Snowflake. That bothered me, but at least he had the guts to say it to my face. Other kids would tease me sometimes for "talking white." That's always annoyed me, the idea that if your subjects and your verbs agree, that's somehow talking white. It's true, though, that there are different styles of speech and I've always been able to code-switch well, even before it was labeled as such. If I'm hanging out with my family on a weekend, I'm probably not talking quite the same way as I do during the week in a primarily white setting. But then neither is anyone: we all have different selves we present to family, friends, colleagues, and strangers, and none is necessarily more authentic than another. In my case, the teasing I endured in high school only made me tougher and more comfortable in my own skin. (I don't want to overplay that teasing, but I felt a twinge of empathy when we did a "Dad's Got This!" segment on Greg Long, a father from the Chicago area whose teenage son, Jimmy, is a passionate competitive dancer. When Jimmy was bullied and even subjected to homophobic slurs from young audience members during a performance, Greg responded by creating a hashtag campaign, #DanceOn, to support male dancers. The message, Greg said, was "Don't stop just because someone thinks you shouldn't." #DanceOn has since morphed into a nonprofit that raises money to fund dance scholarships for boys.)

Ultimately, that's what Mom wanted for me, to feel like I belonged anywhere I wanted to belong. Grandma Florence would sometimes warn against too much assimilation. If I was going out with a group of friends or going to a party where she knew there would be a lot of white people, she'd tell me to be careful, to not let my guard down. It was something we used to joke about in our family, the way that whenever Grandma talked about white people, she would refer to them as W's. She'd say things like, "Be careful, the W's will cut your head off." She was kidding, the way a grandma might tease a kid about the boogeyman, but there was an underlying real concern. Keep in mind that this was a woman who had grown up in the Deep South in the 1930s, at the height of the Jim Crow era. She had seen flaming KKK crosses and worse, so she was naturally suspicious of white people. She and her family lived in a completely segregated society; the only whites they associated with were the people for whom they worked.

Ryan and I grew up in a very different world, but there was still a type of what I call soft racism that remained so endemic you didn't always notice it. For instance, we used to love a barbecue place called Maurice's Piggie Park, which was right around the corner from Grandma Rene's. We'd get dinner from there once or twice a month, often on Fridays as an end-of-the-week treat. Maurice's was a little drive-in where you pulled in and ordered at a window, and they would bring the food out to your car. It wasn't until I was in middle school that I realized, "Wait a minute, we're eating beneath a huge Confederate flag." The restaurant had a big pole out front where they flew it beneath the U.S. and the South Carolina state flags—and I hadn't realized what it really represented, how racist it was, until I was nearly a teenager. My parents should have known; it didn't seem to bother them. Back then, though, people didn't necessarily question those kinds of hate symbols, and I do think it speaks volumes about how far we've come, and relatively quickly, that Confederate iconography is now unwelcome in so many places, especially the South. Not so long ago, it was commonplace—there was a Confederate battle flag flying on the grounds of the state capitol in Columbia until it was finally lowered in 2015, following the shooting at the Mother Emanuel AME Church in Charleston. For years, my family had sat beneath another one eating mustard barbecue, twice a month, thinking nothing of it until we got older and knew better.

THE SUMMER AFTER EIGHTH GRADE WAS a memorable one for me, with two incidents that, in hindsight, really capture my different relationships with my parents. Pops, like a lot of dads, had a knack for biting off more than he could chew when it came to home improvement projects, convincing himself he could do things that he would have been better off paying somebody else to take care of. That year, 1993, as summer was approaching, we started having trouble with the toilets in the house. Pops eventually got a guy to come check the problem out; he said our sewer line was too old and needed to be replaced. Naturally, Pops decided he could do it himself—in part because he was inspired by Joe Visconti, who had replaced his own sewer years before, and in part because he had a teenager at home who was enjoying his summer vacation and thus had lots of free time to help. (Thanks, Joe.)

Pops would finish the third shift at the post office, come home, wake me up, and the two of us would get to work digging up the sewer line from the house to the street and then replacing all the piping. This was all done during the midday June and July heat of South Carolina. Imagine taking a hot shower, not drying off, and instead putting on two layers of clothes—that's what a South Carolina summer is like.

I was out in the sun with Pops for weeks, digging away, and growing more and more pissed at him for being too cheap to hire somebody. (I realize now he didn't have the luxury, like I currently do, of picking up the phone and calling someone for even minor home repairs.) Believe me, these are not pleasant memories, but as with our work on the LeMans, we also enjoyed a sense of comradeship that I appreciated even then—when I wasn't grumbling—and that I appreciate even more now. I suppose resenting your father and at the same time quietly craving his attention is almost the definition of being fourteen. And I did receive a reward when the sewer dig was completed: a pair of black-and-white Reebok Pumps that I desperately wanted for the next school year. To this day, I have never appreciated a pair of shoes more than those high-top Pumps.

Meanwhile that summer, on my off-hours, I'd made friends with a sixteen-year-old young lady who lived around the corner. One thing led to another, and I had one of my earliest sexual encounters. A few weeks later, she called to tell me her period was late and she was convinced she was pregnant. I was beyond terrified. I couldn't sleep. I thought my life was ruined, that I was about to become a statistic. I had no idea how to handle the situation. I certainly didn't feel like I could talk to Mom or Pops about it. Instead, I kept it to myself for as long as I could, until my friend made it clear that we had to do *something*, that I needed to address this. So I went to my aunt Wanda, who was like a big sister to me. She listened without judgment and then said, "You've got to tell your mom"—which of course was the right advice. I had confided in Wanda at Grandma Florence's house; Mom was there that day, too. So I sat her down and explained the predicament as best I could. She began to cry uncontrollably. I started crying, too—and apologizing. And then, almost in an instant, Mom took control. She said she was going to call my friend herself and follow up. I was too scared to object. Mom suspected that she might have been using our relationship to try and get money. Mom also knew that a young girl who was possibly pregnant would need to see a doctor and that she might be too scared to ask her own parents for help.

The next morning, Mom took her for an exam. I was so nervous after Mom left. This was long before cell phones, so I had no idea what was going on. For hours, with what felt like a black hole in the pit of my stomach, I was just waiting for my mother to come home. Finally she walked in the front door. All Mom said was "She's not pregnant." Then she went into the back bedroom and closed the door. That was it: no debrief, no punishment, no lecture about responsibility or morality or birth control. Nothing. That's how delicate things were handled in our family. Mom knew I had learned my lesson. We haven't spoken about it since.

Pops never knew. I asked Mom to not tell him. I'm not sure why. I guess I could have talked to him about it—probably for a lot of boys it would have been more natural to talk to their father in that situation—but my dad and I just didn't have that kind of relationship.

Whatever I did wrong, my mom always had an unrelenting belief in me, so much so that from the time I was fourteen or fifteen, I knew I was going to be successful, whether it was in law, politics, journalism, or something else. I hope that doesn't sound arrogant. It was all due to her faith in me; there was never a question I would excel—she made sure I did. To put it another way, and more crudely: I was afraid to screw up, big-time. I think on occasions she even lived vicariously through me. Maybe that had to do with frustrations with her own life, with her marriage. Whatever the cause, I sensed her pride in me and it drove me.

My dad, on the other hand, wasn't that involved with my academic life, and later I found out perhaps why. My mom told me a story that now makes me cringe. When I was in the first grade, she said, Pops was trying to help me with my homework and I brushed him off with something along the lines of "But, Pops, you didn't go to college. You can't help me with my homework." I was six, and six-year-olds can say a lot of awful things, but still, that must have really hurt him—and the hurt may have stayed with him and shaped our interactions with regards to school. I never had conversations with him about where I was going to college or what I was going to study. Mom filled out all my financial aid forms. Pops came along to help me move in and he showed up for a couple of parents' weekends and graduation. But academics were not something we talked about, not something we had in common. Maybe that drove a wedge between us.

CHAPTER 3

ROLE MODELS, MENTORS, AND THE GHOST

This may strike many people as a terrible thing to say, but as I got older, I started feeling very consciously that I did not want to be like my father, not in any way. For instance, the constant stench of cigarettes in his car, on him, in the house—you were surrounded by it. I was so put off by the smell that aside from one puff during a fraternity initiation, I've never smoked a cigarette in my life. Granted, the same didn't happen with alcohol. I enjoy a drink, especially a good bourbon, but I've never had much of a taste for beer. Children can be just as motivated by negative examples, and that was certainly the case for me. There came a period when I couldn't see past my dad's flaws, when his strengths were invisible to me.

At the same time, maybe subconsciously, I craved having father figures in my life, and I was lucky in that a number of generous and patient men took an interest in me—relatives, teachers, coaches, friends' dads. Men who showed me how I might carry myself in the world. Maybe my need was obvious? At some point, I felt I wasn't going to get it from Pops.

The first of these and one of the most important was my uncle James, Pops's older brother by four years. For most of his career, Uncle James worked as a civil servant in the Department of Labor in Washington, D.C. He would come back to South Carolina for the big holidays, and in our family's eyes, he was the Man. For one thing, he always drove a Cadillac. If you were a black kid growing up in the eighties in South Carolina, there were certain things that were commonly associated with making it in life, and one of those was owning a Cadillac. I thought, *Wow, Uncle James must be raking in a lot of money, always driving a Cadillac.* Of course there are limits on what you can earn in civil service, but he did very well.

Uncle James had a daughter of his own, my cousin Blossom, but he stepped up to fill what he saw as a paternal void in my life, encouraging me academically and socially. When I was in elementary school, he made a contract with me whereby for every A I earned, I would get five or ten bucks; for every B, I got a little less. I would mail a copy of my report card to Uncle James and he would mail me back my earnings. I don't think Pops knew about our deal, and I doubt he would have liked it if he had. I think he saw his older brother living a life that to some extent he wished he could have had. Over the years there were a couple of times when Uncle James tried to talk to Pops about his drinking, to no avail—aside from probably further fueling his resentment.

As I got older, Uncle James supported me in all kinds of ways. When I was fourteen, I sang lead in some songs in a church choir concert and he showed up for it, even though he went to a different church. I could see him in the pew, singing and clapping along, which meant a lot to me. He's a proud member of Kappa Alpha Psi, one of the quintessential African American fraternities, and through him, when I was in high school, I got involved, too. I participated in the Kappa Beautillion, which is like a debutante cotillion for young men, and ended up winning a scholarship for college. During winter break one year I lived with him in D.C. while I interned on Capitol Hill for Senator Fritz Hollings. Uncle James taught me a bit about wine that winter and we had some free-flowing conversations about politics and life. He was treating me somewhat like a peer; it was one of those moments where an adult relative welcomes you to the grown-up table. Uncle James helped open up the world to me in ways my parents couldn't.

On my mom's side of the family, there was Uncle Jake. He was married to Aunt Ella, Mom's sister. Theirs was the house that shared a backyard fence with Grandma Florence's, where I went to play with my cousin Clifton. I was fascinated by Uncle Jake's eager involvement in Cliff's life, which was so different from the dynamic between my father and me. Uncle Jake was Cliff's rec league soccer coach until Cliff started playing club soccer. Together, the two of them were always on the go, to and from soccer practices, games, and tournaments. Cliff was so good he ended up getting an athletic scholarship to the U.S. Naval Academy. Years later, when I was working on the "Dad's Got This!" series for the *Today* show, profiling a group of dads who pitched in backstage with their daughters' dance troupe, or the dad who started a girls' wrestling club when his daughter couldn't find a place to practice the sport, I would be reminded of Uncle Jake and his support of Cliff's passion for soccer.

Uncle Jake even did his best to help me out with my golf game. Early on in my career, I would be invited to participate in charity tournaments—an occupational hazard of being on TV. I didn't know how to play, but I quickly realized that learning would be close to a professional necessity. Uncle Jake loved the game, so he and a friend of his, an older white guy named Willard, took me out a few times to teach me. They tried their damnedest, but I was terrible. I appreciated, though, how patient Uncle Jake was with me, and I've gotten a *little* better since then.

Another thing about Uncle Jake is that he's a big churchgoer. Uncle Pop fell away for a while, but he now worships regularly, too. And Uncle James, who lives in Columbia now, is a deacon for his congregation. In all of them, I saw elements of the type of man that I wanted to be from a young age. You could say that, over the years, I managed to cobble together a role model from different men in my family.

And women. My dad's sister Carrie Mae was a nurse and a big booster when it came to education. Of all his siblings, she was the one he was closest to. She lived in Columbia and we saw her often. She loved to quiz Ryan and me on spelling. She'd ask us to spell a word; if we got it right, she might give us a dollar. It got to the point where we expected to get paid pretty much every time we saw Aunt Carrie Mae, and thanks in no small part to her financial encouragement, I ended up being such a prolific speller that in seventh grade, much to my surprise, I made it to a school district–wide spelling bee. Aunt Carrie Mae helped me prep, but I came up short. To this day, I remember the word I was eliminated on: *license.* (I added an extra *s*: *l-i-s-c-e-n-s-e.*)

Aunt Carrie Mae and I also took a legendary road trip together, when I was ten, to Canton, Ohio, to see the Pro Football Hall of Fame. Not everyone likes to spend hard-won vacation time in Canton, but that was a regular trip for Carrie Mae. She was a huge fan of the sport, and she and Pops enjoyed watching games together. They had something else in common: a habit of driving well below the speed limit. When I was in a car with her, I'd think, *My god, why are we barely moving?* So it took us almost twice as long to get to the Hall of Fame as it should have—and the round trip was 1,100 miles. She originally wanted my dad to go with her, but he made some excuse to get out of going. She still needed a road-trip buddy, so I was drafted. Maybe Pops knew that because she was as careful with her money as he usually was, we'd be eating pretty much nothing but her bologna sandwiches all the way to Canton and back. Limited menu notwithstanding, the trip with Aunt Carrie Mae was truly a highlight of my early years—riding, talking, listening, and visiting parts of the country I'd never seen.

I TOOK AN EVEN MORE MEMORABLE road trip to New York City when I was thirteen, with Aunt Wanda, Grandma Florence, and Wanda's boyfriend, Lindsey, to visit my second cousin Anita, who was the pride and joy of the family in part because she had gone to Yale. (Her mother and Grandma Florence were sisters.) I had been to New York once before, when I was six, but beyond my brief meeting with Grandpa Curtis I didn't have any significant memories of that trip, so this visit was eye-opening for me on many levels.

Anita had grown up in New York and she and her mom lived in the Bronx. The trip took place in 1992. Spike Lee's movie *Malcolm X* had just come out, and it was all anyone was talking about. Anita was woke long before most—she always had a political consciousness and she's spent her career doing good in the nonprofit sector. She either gave me a copy of *The Autobiography of Malcolm X* or told me to buy one, and that book became the first piece of nonfiction I'd ever read cover to cover without its having been assigned in school. I found Malcolm's political and spiritual journey eye-opening and inspiring. Anita also took us to Harlem. I was struck by all the people on the street, especially the sidewalk vendors. That was something you never saw in Columbia. I bought an X hat and a T-shirt and became very militant for about three or four months—black with a very definite capital B.

That was all thanks to Anita, and it marked the first time that I thought deeply about certain matters of race. Going to public school in South Carolina in the 1980s and 90s, you learned about the civil rights movement. You knew who Dr. Martin Luther King Jr., Harriet Tubman, and Booker T. Washington were. But schools didn't spend a lot of time on Malcolm X or the Black Panthers. Our history classes didn't include the Black Power movement—in fact, I think our teachers deliberately shied away from it. Maybe that's why part of me is still drawn to that: not militancy per se, but the idea that when it comes to race, some people have been more willing than others to make waves and buck convention, to not adapt to the norms and expectations of white culture. That's one reason, out of many, why Muhammad Ali is an idol of mine. As you'll see later, another man I admire who cut his own path is Jim Vance, a legendary Washington, D.C., news anchor who would play an important role in my career.

I CAN'T TALK ABOUT SURROGATE FATHERS, role models, and race and not mention Bill Cosby, his disgrace notwithstanding. For me, growing up, there was no TV show more important than *The Cosby Show*. It's difficult to overstate how much kids like me looked up to Theo and Denise, Vanessa and Rudy and Sondra. Just about every black kid that I knew in the 1980s and 90s wanted to be a Cosby kid—we all saw ourselves in that family. I, for one, also yearned for a father like Cliff Huxtable. He didn't need to be a doctor or a lawyer, but I wanted a dad who would come in and read the paper and talk about the news and ask me how my day went. Before *The Cosby Show*, I hadn't seen a character like that on television; there was not a black male father who was a professional, who had a happy, intact family, who lived in a nice big house in New York, who talked about highbrow things, who celebrated art and music. A father you could have a real conversation with. That was all foreign to me, both on TV and at my own dinner table.

The Cosby Show was appointment viewing in our house, at least for me. Thursday nights at eight o'clock, I was in front of our TV. Pops would either be at work or on his way to work, so the show wasn't a thing for him. Mom would watch, but not religiously, not like me. To this day, I contend it's the most consequential sitcom in TV history, hands down. It normalized a black experience that wasn't rooted in shucking and jiving; the Cosby kids weren't like J.J. Evans clowning in the Chicago projects on *Good Times*, mouthing a catchphrase like "Dyn-o-mite!" White kids had idealized TV father figures to look up to for decades, going back to *The Adventures of Ozzie and Harriet, Leave It to Beaver,* and *The Brady Bunch.* For black kids, Dr. Huxtable was something new. That's why, beyond the human cost for all concerned, especially the victims, it was so painful for me—and for so many people—when Bill Cosby was accused and convicted of rape. It was a stain on what he had meant to so many of us growing up.

I was also a big fan of *A Different World,* the *Cosby Show* spin-off set at a fictional HBCU. That series romanticized the HBCU experience so convincingly that when I was a senior in high school I applied to Morehouse College, in Atlanta. I was accepted, too, but we would have had to mortgage the house for me to attend. I got a better scholarship offer from Wofford College, in Spartanburg, South Carolina, so that's where I went. I loved it, too—so much so that I now serve on the school's board of trustees—but I often wonder what my life would have been like had I gone to an all-male, all-black college like Morehouse.

I will say that as much as I've never wanted my race to define me, the older I've gotten, and the more of this country I've seen, and the more of this world I've seen, the more I've realized that unfortunately we still live in a day and age where so much of who we are is defined by the social construct that is race. It's wearying and sometimes depressing. All the same, my blackness has probably helped me as much as it's hurt me. I've had mentors in my life who, I believe, took an interest in me at least in part to help assuage their white guilt. Frankly, and sadly, there have also been points in my life where, without realizing it at the time, I probably served as a token. So it's complicated. It was complicated when I was growing up, maybe more than I realized, and it still is.

THROUGH MIDDLE SCHOOL AND INTO HIGH school, Pops continued to try and parent me in his intermittent way. When I was in sixth or seventh grade, I decided it would be a good idea to make a few extra bucks by going around the neighborhood offering to clean up yards and cut grass, using Pops's lawn mower—which was usually half broken and required almost as much work as the LeMans. To his credit, though, he allowed me to borrow it.

I was getting twenty bucks a lawn—good money then. Occasionally, though, I would bite off more than I could chew. Maybe there would be a particularly massive yard or an unusually messy or overgrown lawn. For whatever reason, it might be getting late in the afternoon and Pops would drive by and see that I was struggling, so he would get out and help. He didn't even ask. He just jumped in and started working. Maybe he'd use the Weedwacker while I was cutting the lawn, or vice versa. Sometimes, when I had to trim hedges, a tricky operation, he'd assist. In hindsight, his happening to drive by so many times seems a little *too* coincidental: I suspect he was checking up on me. I resented it at the time. I had a lot of pride, and having him help was a tacit admission that I couldn't do the job by myself. But the reality was that I *did* need his help a fair number of times, which is something hard for a twelve- or thirteen-year-old boy to admit, though I appreciated the fact that he wouldn't take a cut of my fee.

One afternoon two years later, after I had gotten my learner's permit, he let me drive the LeMans home from one of my aunts' houses. We were on Interstate 20. Pops was in the passenger seat, drunk and asleep. I was driving in the slow lane, behind a guy who was crawling along at something like 45 miles per hour. So I put on my turn signal, looked in the rearview and side-view mirrors, checked my blind spot, and moved into the left lane, just as I'd been taught in driver training. *Textbook*. I accelerated to pass, reaching the speed limit of 60 miles per hour; then I signaled again and moved back into the right lane. Still textbook. But I swerved a little awkwardly, and Pops suddenly snapped to and yelled, "Damn it, what the hell are you doing?" Then he took his left hand and thumped me in the chest—while I'm *driving*, mind you. "Pops," I yelped, "what was that for? I'm not speeding." He wasn't having it. "You're driving too fast. And if you're going to drive that fast, you're not going to drive my car." I thought to myself, *Who is this man who thinks driving 60 on the interstate is unacceptable?* But I slowed down all the same and did a miserable 55 all the way home.

As I said, Pops, like his sister Carrie Mae, was always a notoriously slow driver, often below the speed limit, *never* above it. His drinking and driving notwithstanding, I guess he was worried about our safety. Or, I sometimes wondered, was his concern the hazard of a potential DUI or DWB (Driving While Black)?

It turned out the answer is none of the above. "I don't need to hurry," he told me recently. "If I got somewhere to go, I leave in time enough to get there—fifteen, twenty minutes before time. I don't like to go no place and have to rush out. I lived that."

SETTING ASIDE THE EPISODE WHERE MY mom spanked me over a report card, I tended to be a "just good enough" student. What I was superb at in class was talking—in turn, out of turn, incessantly. That was a constant refrain in parent-teacher conferences: *your son talks a lot*. Out of class, too; I just always enjoyed engaging with people. (My mom told me that even when I was a toddler I wouldn't stop chattering.) It wasn't until the second semester of my sophomore year in high school that I developed what you might call a legitimate intellectual curiosity to complement my garrulousness. I did well enough in English, history, politics, and government, but I had no patience for math or science, having no interest in subjects where there was only one correct answer to any question. I liked debate and discussion and gray areas; even in high school I had an ability, even a desire, to see all sides of a host of issues. That's one reason I've been able to be a reasonably successful journalist.

Over the years, I had a number of teachers who shaped and molded me in important ways. One of my favorites was also one of the most influential: my third-grade teacher, Mr. Brandon. One of our assignments in his class was to make a music video and weave in historical figures. Two friends and I chose the song "Part of My Design," by Kid Creole and the Coconuts, which name-checks a lot of historical figures. My friends played Robert F. Kennedy and Dr. Martin Luther King Jr., while I put on a white bathrobe to play

Mahatma Gandhi. I can't remember what we actually did in the video; hopefully no old VHS will ever surface to remind me.

That was the kind of teacher Mr. Brandon was. He really encouraged learning through creativity. I got another chance in front of the camera in middle school, when our English teacher gave us an assignment to write and shoot video book reports. My friends and I did *The Call of the Wild* by Jack London. That may have been when I first realized I enjoyed being on camera. I kept thinking, *How cool is this?*

Around that same time, the school district decided it was going to produce an election-night TV special. This was November 1992, when Bill Clinton was challenging George H.W. Bush, the incumbent president. The idea for the show was pretty basic: kids would announce the election results as they came in. The district wanted it to be a show for students, and they wanted students to produce it and star in it. I can't remember whether I had to audition or not, but I was selected. So there I was on election night, on TV, calling races on the Richland County public access channel. Again, I found I really loved being on camera.

Afterwards, kids told me they'd seen me on TV, but what I enjoyed even more was hearing from adults, who said things like, "Hey, I saw you last night. You did a really good job." That made me feel like I'd made an actual impression on my small corner of the world. Obviously, adults weren't going to tell a fifth grader that they thought he sucked, but I would like to think that maybe I was a bit of a natural. Keep in mind, I had spent my entire life up until that point running my mouth. This was just more talking, on camera.

If my parents had any reaction to my first live TV appearance, I don't recall it. I doubt Pops saw me; he was probably at work. Mom definitely didn't. She had to drive me to the studio and wait while I did it. I'm sure she was proud of me, but on the whole, my parents didn't do much of what I call *praise heaping*. Ryan and I knew we were loved, but it wasn't like Mom and Pops were hugging us every day and telling us how great we were. We got a lot of support, but we didn't get hosannas, which has probably served us well.

THE FIRST NATIONAL NEWS EVENT I can remember in any detail is the Space Shuttle Challenger disaster. That tragedy took place on January 28, 1986, when I was six years old and in first grade. Like kids across America we watched the launch and explosion in class that morning but I didn't really process what had happened. Pops picked me up from school that afternoon, then went back to his bedroom to sleep. I turned on the TV in the living room, probably expecting *The Flintstones* or *Tom and Jerry*, but instead saw ongoing coverage of the explosion and its aftermath. Mom was still at work, so I was left trying to make sense of it all by myself. I still didn't quite understand what had happened. To that point, in my experience, space travel had been reliable, shuttle flights routine. I didn't realize that the astronauts were dead, but I knew something terrible had happened—and I knew this was not like anything I'd seen on TV before. I was scared and upset. I cried.

In hindsight, that clearly wasn't a good thing, my watching the Challenger coverage and not having an adult there to comfort me and help me understand. Then again, maybe the struggle to make sense of the tragedy helped hook me on the news, on trying to explain things and put them in context for other people. Years later, ironically, I had a chance to do exactly that when I was up for a job, early in my career. One thing broadcast news bosses typically do as part of an audition is force you to handle a simulated breaking news event. You'll be doing a mock newscast and a producer will suddenly get in your ear and say, "Okay, such and such has just happened. Here are a few facts. We need you to vamp for two minutes about it." In one of my auditions, the simulated breaking news was the Challenger explosion. So that came full circle for me.

Nowadays, my dad is a voracious TV news consumer, but when I was growing up neither he nor Mom paid it much more than passing attention. Watching the news was something I came to on my own, and as I got older, I grew more and more fascinated by it, to the point that by eighth grade I was acing the weekly current events contest run by my history teacher, Mr. Waites. Mostly I watched local news, and mainly the evening news on WIS-TV, the NBC affiliate in Columbia, South Carolina—where I would later get my first paying job—but occasionally I would switch over to WLTX-TV, the CBS affiliate. I watched every night and knew all the anchors. I'm not sure why I was so obsessed with local news, but I suppose the kinds of stories—robberies and car wrecks and fires and state fairs—were more interesting to my young self than congressional budget fights or stock market plunges.

I had had a closeup look at the WIS news operation when I appeared on the *Mr. Knozit Show*. That was the station's Saturday-morning children's program. A guy named Joe Pinner, who was also the WIS weatherman, played the host, Mr. Knozit. He would show old cartoons, bring on a special guest who would appeal to kids, like a firefighter or a cop, and ask all the boys and girls in the audience questions like what they wanted to be when they grew up. The show had started in 1963 and was still going strong in the eighties; for decades, if you were a kid growing up in or around Columbia, you were desperate to be on the *Mr. Knozit Show*, and if you were one of the lucky kids who made it into the audience, that was a big, big deal, accompanied by serious bragging rights. The show was shot at WIS in the same studio where the nightly news was broadcast. Seeing that set and all the lights and cameras, getting a sense of how the TV sausage is made, had a big impact on me. Often, when people not in the business visit a TV set, they find it disillusioning—smaller, flimsier, much less glamorous than they imagined. For me, it was thrilling and alluring.

As a budding journalist, I got my first big "break," if you will, when I was fifteen, one afternoon when I was home from school watching something on WIS. A commercial announced that the station was looking for a high school reporter as part of a journalism program for teenagers called Our Generation Reporters. The notion was that you would work as a correspondent with an established producer on stories that were of particular interest to high school kids; this was the station's attempt at reaching a young, hip audience.

The ad said that they would be holding auditions at the Richland Fashion Mall. I asked my mom, the granter of all significant permissions in our house, if I could go. She said yes. But here's an amazing thing: in South Carolina, in those days, if you had a learner's permit you could drive during daylight hours without an adult, and Pops gave me permission to drive to the mall by myself in the LeMans, which felt like a serious sign of respect on his part, though it's possible Mom was too busy to drive me in her car and he simply didn't want to. Happily, the LeMans didn't break down. I made it to the mall in one piece, and somehow did well enough in the audition to get picked—which was really the beginning of my career. A few weeks later, when I walked into the WIS newsroom for the first time, I was wide-eyed. Men and women I had watched on TV all of my life, local news legends—including Joe Pinner of *Mr. Knozit* fame, who ended up becoming a friend—were sitting right there, within arm's reach, writing scripts, working the phones. For me, it was magic.

I loved the work, too, and even won an award for a profile I did of my AP World History teacher, Mr. Fanning, another influential figure for me. He was the kind of teacher who would dress in garb from the time period to help teach you about the Shang Dynasty, or bring in Turkish food when you were studying the Ottoman empire. He went out of his way to bring lessons to life. The award I won for profiling Mr. Fanning was given by the state chapter of the Associated Press, and if I wasn't already hooked on broadcast journalism, that recognition sealed it.

It's funny, though, when people ask about how my career started and I think back to auditioning for Our Generation Reporters, I can't remember the audition itself. I can't remember the news story that they asked me to talk about. I can't remember who interviewed me. What I remember, like it was yesterday, is driving the Pontiac Le-Mans by myself to Richland Fashion Mall, and the pride I felt that Pops had trusted me with it. I wouldn't go so far as to say it was a rite of passage, but that car just symbolized so much to me—for good or bad, it was the centerpiece of my relationship with him.

THE SAME SUMMER I STARTED WORKING at WIS, a story in the local news hit close to home, tragically and horrifically so. It involved a friend, Brandon Vinson, who had lived two streets over from me. When we were younger, Brandon and I played Little League together and became good friends. He had a little sister named Megan who was about the same age as Ryan, and they were friends, too. We were in and out of each other's houses a lot—the Vinsons had an aboveground pool, so that was a big attraction. In middle school, they moved to the country, to a small town called Red Bank in Lexington County, about thirty minutes outside Columbia, but Brandon and I kept in touch from time to time.

One night in 1995, when we were both in high school, I was

watching the WIS newscast and there was a breaking report with a full screen shot of Brandon's face, followed by video from a crime scene. It was awful. Brandon, who was fifteen, had been killed in what was described as a ritualistic murder. His body, hands bound by baling twine, had been found in an old chicken coop on an abandoned farm, about fifteen miles from the grocery store in Red Bank where he'd been working and was last seen, three days before. His head had been bludgeoned and he was stabbed seventy-two times. I don't even know how to describe my reaction. The fact that something so horrible had happened to a friend—it was just unthinkable. I was overwhelmed.

It was months before there was an arrest, and the case gripped our community. Since it involved someone I knew, it was probably the first news story where I followed every twist and turn. The investigation got off to a bad start with a mess of a crime scene: a lot of evidence had been washed away by rain, and the murder weapon was never found. As the hunt for the killer or killers dragged on, it bothered me the way the many TV news crews and other reporters and photographers hounded Brandon's family as they grieved, angling for any sort of nugget to advance the story. I experienced that firsthand one afternoon at the funeral home, when there was an opportunity for Brandon's friends to pay their respects to his family. We were in a long line, moving slowly, and a reporter and a cameraman were filming us and trying to find anyone who would talk to them. They were from WIS, and even though I was working at the station as an Our Generation Reporter, I thought what they were doing was detestable, pestering people who were grieving the loss of a teenager. A lot of other people in line felt the same way. We treated the news team like pariahs.

So there I was at the age of sixteen, disgusted with a reporter who was hounding the friends and family of a murder victim, not knowing that in a few years this would be something I would be called upon to do on a semi-regular basis. Those are some of the most difficult assignments I've ever had, doing exactly what that reporter and cameraman were doing that day, trying to get people to humanize a loved one who's been lost in a shattering, inconceivable way. When I was working at WIS full time as a reporter in the early 2000s, at the height of the Iraqi and Afghan wars, I was often tasked with knocking on the doors or calling the homes of soldiers who'd been killed in action to see if a mother or father or sister or brother or husband or wife would talk to me about the person they'd just lost. It's always been one of the worst parts of the job.

Brandon's family never really got justice, only a long, strange, and inconclusive legal drama. A seventeen-year-old boy, a drifter of sorts, was eventually arrested in Arizona and charged with Brandon's murder; he had allegedly confessed to some friends, divulging aspects of the killing known only to police. There was no physical evidence tying him to the crime, however, and for reasons the authorities have never explained, he ended up spending ten years in the Lexington County jail before finally offering what's called an Alford plea, in which he conceded the strength of the evidence against him and pled guilty while continuing to assert his innocence. (An Alford plea is different from a no contest plea, in which a defendant asserts neither guilt nor innocence but acknowledges the likelihood of being found guilty.)

He was sentenced to ten more years in prison and was released in 2015. Brandon's relatives, whom I still keep in touch with, are convinced to this day that the wrong person was charged with the murder and that there may have been two assailants. At one point, a *Dateline* producer and I even looked into doing a story on the case after the family discovered some new evidence that they thought might be strong enough to get the case reopened, but their leads ended up being inconclusive.

MY RELATIONSHIP WITH MY DAD DETERIORATED considerably during these middle school and high school years. Some of that was probably due to normal teenager stuff on my part. But his drinking was getting worse, and a second addiction had entered his and our lives.

In 1986, the South Carolina state legislature passed a thick and complicated budget bill with an obscure provision, buried deep within, which legalized payouts on video poker machines. It was barely noticed at the time, but within a few years, gambling on video poker became a huge industry in South Carolina. The game machines began turning up in bars, restaurants, convenience stores, liquor stores, arcades, road stops, gas stations, bowling alleys—pretty much anywhere you could think of, aside from churches and schools. The way this typically worked was an establishment would have its usual wares or services up front, and in the back, you would find one or two or more video poker machines. You put in a dollar or five or ten, and you could play a series of virtual poker hands against the machine, no raises or bluffing, just trying to beat the computer's hand.

At its peak, in 1999, this was a $3 billion business. By one estimate, there were machines in fully a quarter of South Carolina's retail businesses. In 1997, *The Wall Street Journal* wrote that "neon signs offering 'Video Games' are now as ubiquitous as sermon signs before churches"—and in my home state, that's saying something. People called video poker the crack cocaine of gambling. It was a unique scourge, one that was largely unregulated; what regulations there were, like a supposed limit on the number of machines an establishment could have, were easily and widely circumvented.

Like far too many South Carolinians, my dad got hooked, playing at a liquor store about a mile from our house called Tom's Party Shop. Every other Friday, when Pops would get paid, he'd go to the bank, cash his check, then go to Tom's, where he'd buy himself a Budweiser tallboy and then squander hundreds of dollars on video poker, sometimes close to his entire paycheck. It got to the point where, on Fridays, my mother would drive over to Tom's and try to stanch the flow. While Ryan and I sat in the car, she would march in and negotiate as much of his paycheck as she could to pay bills. I didn't realize until years later that a significant part of his savings had been squandered on video poker. At one point, Mom had to get a second job, working as a cashier at Phar-Mor—a big CVS-like pharmacy. It was bananas, her taking that job, on top of raising two young children and working full time as an elementary school teacher. But she had to make ends meet and Pops was dropping the ball. I was a bit awestruck at the way Mom was busting her hump to help us. As I saw it, she was adding, Pops was subtracting. She held down two jobs for a couple of years, until it became just too much for her, and she quit Phar-Mor. Ryan and I missed the free video rentals we'd come to enjoy on the weekends, but we understood.

Pops had always enjoyed gambling. He told me a cousin had started him shooting dice for money when he was twelve or thirteen, but in adulthood he'd limited himself to small-stakes card games and playing craps in the Cut. His video poker fixation was different. Sometimes Mom would send me into Tom's Party Shop to ask him for money for groceries or to buy a pair of shoes, or for some random excuse she'd invented just to get money so he wouldn't waste it. The scene at Tom's was sad. I'd walk in and the guy at the register would point me to the back. He knew my brother and me, and he knew our dad was blowing our family's paycheck—not that this knowledge prompted him to get rid of video poker. So I would walk past the beer, wine, and liquor to find Pops slouched hypnotized in front of a machine with a cigarette in one hand, his other hand mindlessly tapping the buttons, his trusty Budweiser always at his side. I could usually tell right away by his mood how he was doing. I'd stand and watch him play a few hands, and then he'd either decide to give me a few bucks or send me on my way with nothing. If I caught him after he'd won big, I might get out of there with a couple of twenty-dollar bills in my pocket, or even a hundred. But more often than not, he was losing. His twin addictions fueled each other: the more he drank, the worse his gambling decisions became.

He became such a fixture at the back of Tom's that even my friends noticed. Kids would tell me, "Hey, I saw your dad up at Tom's." For a number of years, if he wasn't at the house or at work, that's where he was. What probably saved him, and may ultimately have saved my parents' marriage, was that video poker was finally banned in South Carolina, in 2000, because it had destroyed so many families. There had been a notorious case, three years earlier, when a ten-day-old baby girl died after her mother left her alone in a hot car for seven hours to play, which became a rallying cry for anti-video-poker activists. Following several failed attempts, the legislature finally passed a bill that put an end to it. Pops was grateful, which might sound odd, but we had talked about the issue a couple of times while the legislation was making its way through to the general assembly, and he was rooting for video poker to be outlawed even as he kept playing—that's how addictive it is. His openness about that took me by surprise, but he knew he had a problem and it appeared as if he knew he couldn't stop on his own.

He had had some help that I didn't know about. He told me recently that Vince Roundtree, our next-door neighbor, came to the house one day and gave Pops "a talking to" about his gambling. "I didn't quit right then," he said, "but Vince put some thoughts in my head. He said gambling wasn't beneficial and wasn't right, which I already knew. But sometimes you need to get a second opinion—or not really an opinion but some talking-to. Some people know they need help. They just need someone to show them right from wrong, I guess." He told me he thought he would have had enough willpower to quit video poker even if the legislature hadn't banned it. "They got them lottery tickets now and they're just as bad as them doggone poker machines, but I don't buy any of them."

"You've never bought a lottery ticket?"

"No, not one."

"Never?"

"Never. Not one. Because it's gambling."

"But you gambled for at least forty years!"

He laughed. "What do you mean? There's a stopping point some-place. Just because you used to do that doesn't mean you still have to do it."

THAT CONFIDENCE AND SELF-BELIEF WAS IN the future. At the time, Pops was spiraling downward. Grief was another factor. Grandma Rene died in 1995, at the age of seventy-eight. She had Alzheimer's and her health had been in decline for a number of years before that, including a bout with colon cancer—a disease that would later cast a dark shadow over the family.

I don't know when she was diagnosed with Alzheimer's, but there was an episode in the early nineties when her dementia be-came noticeable to Ryan and me. We were with Mom at Grandma Rene's for one of our Sunday dinners. Grandma would do all the cooking in the morning, then heat things up after church. The menu was close to ritualized, but in recent months she had started forgetting to make certain dishes, and the quality of her cooking had begun to slide a bit as well. We wrote that off to her getting older—after all, this was a woman well into her seventies still making elaborate family dinners on a weekly basis. Then, one Sunday, we were sitting in the den when we heard this clanging and clamor coming from the kitchen. Grandma was trying to pry her microwave door open with a butter knife; she had forgotten how to press the latch to open it. I was eleven or twelve, and in that moment, I knew she wasn't the same woman.

It got worse quickly. Not long after the microwave incident, she was talking about some money in the house that had gone missing. She moved on to some other topic, then brought up the money again. This happened a couple more times. Then out of the blue, she started accusing Ryan of taking the money, asking him questions in an accusatory tone. He was only five or six. That's when we all acknowledged there was a problem.

My dad took his mother's decline hard. He was so close to her, and she was one of the few people who could really reach him, not just talk to him but connect with him. He was very much on edge where she was concerned in the years leading up to her death. One afternoon following the Sunday-dinner episodes, when it was becoming apparent Grandma was not going to get better, I was in my room when Pops asked me to handle a chore. Apparently I didn't jump to it quickly enough. He stormed back into my room a minute later and started screaming at me. He was angry in a harsh, visceral way that I had not seen before. I remember connecting the dots, understanding even in the moment that whatever his tirade was supposedly about wasn't what it was actually about. It wasn't the chore; it was Grandma's health.

Toward the end, she was hospitalized. I was old enough that I could go to visit her by myself, and the nurses would occasionally let me spend the night. One time I was asleep in the recliner in her room when I woke up to noise and confusion. Grandma Rene had forgotten where she was and why she was there, and, determined to leave, had started taking all the needles and tubes out of her arms. There was blood everywhere. That may have been the last time I spent the night.

My mom saved the eulogy for Grandma that I wrote out in longhand and somehow managed to read aloud in church. Standing over her casket in the church that had been her home for decades, I talked about the pain she had suffered, but then I turned to happier memories: her devotion to her church and our family. "I remember sitting at her kitchen table and waiting to eat. I remember the fried chicken, stew beef and rice, the ham, collard greens, macaroni 'n' cheese, potato salad, cornbread, and the love. . . . I remember the smile of satisfaction on my grandmother's face as I knocked out plate after delicious plate. I remember those four words that she would say after every plate: Have you had enough?" On the page my mom saved, that last word is blurred by what look like several tearstains.

My father was a wreck, as you'd expect. Grandma's funeral was the first time I remember seeing him cry, or really express any kind of profound emotion. Now that he's sober, he's much more like me— he'll puddle up at the drop of a hat. But back then, showing emotion wasn't his way. The funeral aside, he grieved his mother the way he handled so many other issues in his life: by drinking.

NOT SURPRISINGLY, DURING THOSE YEARS, THERE was a significant increase in the tension between my parents. A marriage that had been something of a cold war turned hotter, and they would get into some pretty intense fights—not physical, but with a lot of screaming at each other. There had always been some of that, but there was a lot more when I was in middle school and high school.

When they would really go at it, I'd usually hide out in my room. There were a couple of times, though, where I stood up to Pops. He might be drunk and saying awful things to my mom, even threatening physical abuse. You get to be thirteen or fourteen, you're not going to let someone talk to your mother like that. I would jump up and shout something like, "Okay, Pops, why don't you go ahead and try?" Or "Let's see what happens if you do." He and I never got into physical fights, but a couple of times we got close.

Once, when I was in my late teens, he said something that stayed with me. We were arguing when he told me, "You're like the rest of them. You think you're better than me." That was something he used to say to my mom when they were fighting, and it was something I'd heard him say about other people—Pops definitely had an inferiority complex as well as a chip on his shoulder—but it was the first and only time he said it to me. I don't remember my response, but I do know that by that point, I was damn well sure that yes, I didn't want to end up like him. So if that meant that I thought I was better than he was, then maybe I did.

The older I got, the angrier I got at Pops—and the more I became embarrassed by him, at least where my friends were concerned. When I was younger, he would sometimes shoot the breeze with the neighborhood kids when they came over. He could be funny, and he'd give my buddies a good ribbing about this or that. Granted, some of that was the alcohol talking, but I appreciated he was making an effort. Once in a while he'd come out back and shoot baskets with us, a Newport hanging out of one side of his mouth. He'd say something like "Karl Malone at the top of the key" or "Larry Bird from downtown," and launch a shot. Mostly the ball missed the basket, in which case he liked to say, referencing Malone's nickname, "Guess they were right. The Mailman doesn't deliver on Sundays." He was funny and game and we'd laugh.

All that changed. By the time I was in high school, it wasn't so much the drinking and the gambling in and of themselves that bothered me as it was the fact that he was never around, never a part of my social or school life. Everyone knew I had a father. It wasn't like he was dead or in prison or sick. He wasn't an invalid. He had absented himself. In fact, he was spotted so rarely in public—aside from playing video poker at Tom's—that one of my friends started calling him the Ghost, which became my father's nickname among my friends. On the rare day someone happened to see him out and about, they might say something like, "I saw the Ghost driving home from work in the LeMans this morning," as if that fleeting glimpse were remarkable. The nickname really bugged me.

Most of my other friends, their dads were present. I had written mine off. It got to a point where I thought, *Oh, damn it to hell. I got a dad, but I don't really have a dad.* He *was* like a ghost: there, but not there.

CHAPTER 4

COLLEGE, CLIMBING THE LADDER, AND LOVE

To this day, I don't know how my parents did it, but they put me through college. When I started my freshman year in 1997, Wofford College cost over $20,000 a year. My dad was then probably making somewhere between $45,000 and $50,000 with overtime, my mom $30,000. I had some scholarship money and a financial aid package, and I took out loans, but Mom and Pops really made college possible for me, paying a big chunk out of their own pockets, from savings. Keep in mind that my dad was still hooked on video poker, so they really had to scrape the money together.

Wofford is a small liberal arts college located in Spartanburg, South Carolina, 90 miles from Columbia. It's much more diverse now, but when I entered, I was one of only sixty or so black students out of a student body of 1,150 kids. And of those sixty African Americans, only about ten of us weren't on athletic scholarships. In that sense it felt like an extension of my high school experiences in Model UN and Key Club: I was comfortable in a mostly white environment, yet I was well aware of my minority status.

One thing was new for me: I had never lived intimately with white people before. My freshman roommate was a guy named Ian with really long hair who listened to a lot of Widespread Panic, Grateful Dead, and Phish. *That* was probably my biggest social challenge freshman year, having to listen to endless jam bands. When you hear enough of it—and freshman year I heard way more than enough—it all sounds the same.

I looked into joining Kappa Alpha Psi, Uncle James's fraternity, since I was more or less a legacy, but it turned out there were only two or three Kappas in Wofford's tiny chapter. Kappa Alpha Psi barely had a presence on campus, and my primary motivations in considering Greek life were (1) having something to do on the weekends and (2) meeting girls. I ended up rushing a mostly white fraternity, Kappa Sigma. I worried I had let Uncle James down, but he never said anything about it. I've never forgotten the scholarship I got from Kappa Alpha Psi, and that's one reason why every year when Uncle James asks for support for the fraternity's charity golf tournament, I never hesitate to give.

It turned out the fraternity I rushed was more than mostly white: a friend and I were, in fact, the first black guys to pledge Kappa Sigma at Wofford. I didn't know that until we were well along in the process and someone told us what a big deal us joining was. Not that I had asked. I was obviously aware that all the actives were white, but I had assumed that by the late 1990s there had to have been a black guy in the fraternity at some point. I didn't regret joining, though. In fact I had a great time and made lifelong friends. I even became the chapter vice-president. The real problem was that Kappa Sigma was another hotbed of Widespread Panic, Grateful Dead, and Phish fans. That became my biggest gripe with Wofford: not that the students were homogeneous, but that they listened to awful music. (I have since made my peace with jam bands and will confess to enjoying a Grateful Dead tune from time to time.)

As for academics, I have to confess I struggled mightily my first semester. Keep in mind that my parents had been Stalinist in their approach to how we were reared; that is to say, the Melvin children weren't afforded a lot of liberties. To this point in life, I'd never smoked weed and my experience with alcohol had been fairly limited, starting with a surreptitious beer on a Key Club excursion. So when I finally set foot on campus at Wofford, I felt like it was game on—women, booze, no curfew, freedom! By Christmas I was on academic probation. It didn't help that I was surrounded by like-minded people: there was a large group of us from my freshman dorm who'd had much the same experience that first semester; the others have since become doctors and lawyers, but for a few months in the fall of 1997, it was touch and go as far as our college careers went.

This prompted a rare intervention from my father. As usual with Pops, it wasn't a long conversation. He simply made it clear in no uncertain terms that he was disappointed in my academic performance, that he hadn't sent me to Wofford to drop out. I doubt he'd actually seen my grades; Mom probably told him I was floundering. But he was the one who dressed me down, and as with the cable porn bill, he made it stick. My grades started improving, though it wasn't until second semester sophomore year when I really mastered the collegiate work-life balance.

I MAJORED IN GOVERNMENT AND WAS thinking about a career in politics or law, but eventually decided neither was right for me.

Instead I started focusing on journalism and managed to create a stir with an interview I did for a prospective Wofford TV station some friends and I were hoping to launch. My subject was a campus character everyone knew by sight, since he was always dressed head to foot in black. One day, when I was sitting with some of my fraternity brothers in the cafeteria, he walked by our table and someone said, "Hey, there's the neo-Nazi!" The rest of us were like, "What are you talking about? *That* guy's a neo-Nazi?" It turned out he was indeed, complete with a website and a pseudo–storm trooper organization he'd founded. I of course immediately thought, "What a great get for the TV station—an exclusive sit-down with the campus fascist!" His name was Davis Wolfgang Hawke. The only problem: I was somehow going to have to persuade him to do an interview with me. How likely that was, I wasn't sure, but I approached him one day and he readily agreed to talk to me—for a neo-Nazi he was perfectly friendly. We did the interview in my dorm room; I felt it went well. Somehow, though, word got out and when the administration got wind of the story, they were very unhappy about it—and about the potential bad publicity. After some back and forth, they agreed to run the unedited video in a public setting and then conduct a conversation about it; they wanted to turn it into a teachable moment. At the time I was furious. I saw this as a complete suppression of my First Amendment rights. In hindsight, though, I think it was probably wise to give the interview more context—I wasn't yet an experienced enough journalist to push back against some of Davis's more ridiculous assertions. (One thing I didn't know at the time was that he had changed his name: he was born Andrew Britt Greenbaum to a Jewish father and gentile mother. He later changed his name again, to Jesse James, and moved to British Columbia, where in 2017 his body was found shot to death in a burned out S.U.V. It took three years to identify him.)

Between junior and senior years, I landed a summer job as an associate producer for the morning news show at WIS, where they knew me from my stint in high school as an Our Generation Reporter. The program was called *WIS Sunrise,* and my assignment was writing copy for farm news and cyber news stories—definitely an Odd Couple as beats go. Pretty soon, though, I knew in my gut that this was what I wanted to do professionally. I fell in love with the newsroom, with the relentless pace, with the variety of stories, with the energy. It helped, too, that I was working in a newsroom in the town I grew up in. A lot of the men and women we were covering were people I actually knew. I knew a couple of city council members. I knew the mayor. That all helped. I also took a couple of classes in journalism and broadcast production at the University of South Carolina that summer.

I graduated from Wofford in May 2001. Mom, Pops, Ryan, Grandma Florence, and Aunt Carrie Mae were all there for the ceremony. Pops put his arm around me and said he was proud of me. I'm sure he'd done that before, from time to time, but that's the first time I remember *feeling* his pride in me.

Two weeks later I rejoined WIS. I was hired as a field video photographer—a cameraman, to laypeople—with the idea that I'd learn the ropes and eventually progress to shooting and producing my own segments.

I moved into Grandma Rene's house in Cayce, which my parents had inherited. It was close to the TV station and I couldn't really afford rent, so my parents let me live there with a college buddy. He was white and would frequently talk about how he felt like the only white person in town, since in our neighborhood he never saw anyone else who looked like him. I would think, *Welcome to my world. This is what it's like to be me.*

When we first moved in, I was struck by how little the neighborhood had changed from my childhood. A lot of the same people were still there, like the little old lady two doors up who used to sweep the dust back and forth in the street. And I couldn't throw a stone without hitting someone I was related to, either by blood or marriage. For instance, Aunt Carrie Mae's son's mother-in-law lived just around the corner from me. One night I was in the checkout line at the local Piggly Wiggly supermarket, and being right out of college, I wasn't managing my money very well. At the register I realized I didn't have enough to pay for my groceries. My dad's cousin Wilson Dantzler happened to be behind me in line and gave me a twenty. (As I wrote this, I realized I never paid him back.)

At Grandma Rene's, I stayed in the room where Mr. Ed had slept and where he had died. The house needed a lot of work, and unfortunately we had to rely on Pops to fix stuff—he was essentially the super. He wouldn't always respond quickly when something was broken, which frustrated my roommate, but I was just grateful that we were able to live there for nearly free, since after two years I was able to save up enough money to buy my first house. It was a big step up in lifestyle: two stories, three bedrooms, two-and-a-half baths. It was in downtown Columbia, not far from the station. But an even more important selling point for young Craig Melvin was the fact that the house came equipped with a deck and a hot tub; it soon fulfilled its destiny as a major party pad. I was proud to own my own place, but you have to remember this was the early 2000s, when anyone could buy a house with two paystubs and a driver's license.

At WIS, one of my very first assignments was a story about Burger King. The company was shutting down several of its restaurants in the Columbia area. My assignment was to go out and shoot footage of the Burger Kings that were closing—images of the signs and doors and whatever else that could be cut into the story as needed. Very basic stuff. So I took the camera out and, not lacking confidence, I started getting fancy with my shots—tilting, panning, zooming. Basically, I was shooting my happy ass off for the better part of an afternoon.

I brought the tape back to the station, very excited to get a look at what I'd done, and immediately popped it into a tape deck. But there was something wrong with the deck or maybe—I started to get a little anxious—the tape. I asked the chief photographer, a guy named Randy Johnson, to help me figure out what was wrong. He wasn't sure what the issue was, so he told me to get my camera, saying "Just walk me through exactly what you did while you were shooting." So I did. I showed him just how I'd operated the camera, precisely as I'd been taught. I finished the demonstration, and Randy said, "Well, there's one problem, Craig. You never pressed record."

Talk about rookie mistakes. It turned out I wasn't a very good photographer. And once I started producing, it didn't take long for me to realize that I wasn't very good at that, either. Producing television news requires an attention to detail that I did not possess back then. It also requires ceding a certain amount of control to your reporters and anchors. I would have a vision in my head of how I thought a given newscast should flow. Then I would get in the control room, and five minutes into the show, my vision would be shot to hell—which was hard for me. So somewhat by default, I became a reporter.

My first regular on-camera assignment was doing what we called "Craig Cam" segments for the morning show. I would go out every morning and broadcast live from a different location—it might be a promotion for the state fair or some trade show coming to town. During each show I would typically have five or six "hits," as we called them, where I'd be on air for two minutes or so. Craig Cams weren't great journalism, but they were popular and got me noticed. All that incessant talking that had gotten me in trouble in school was starting to pay off professionally.

Somehow I thought it would be a good idea to do a Craig Cam from the post office processing plant in Dixiana, where Pops was then working, to show folks what a big mail operation was like. We hyped it up and promoted the fact that I was going to talk to my dad. The morning show aired from five until seven, which was toward the end of his shift, so I planned to interview him for the last hit. He and I had talked about it and he seemed gung ho. But then, when it was time to go live, he was suddenly nowhere to be found. I was dumbfounded. He'd gone completely MIA.

I covered by grabbing the local post office spokesman, who was on hand. But Pops had left me hanging on live TV. The thing was, he was still there at the facility: he had deliberately hidden out in the restroom or the break room. I think in the end he felt uncomfortable talking on live TV. It's possible he'd been drinking, which at that point he'd begun doing on the job sometimes, but instead of telling me he wanted to back out, he ghosted me. I was furious and embarrassed. I never confronted him about it, though, until recently. When I asked, "Pops, what the heck happened there?" he claimed that we had had a misunderstanding, that he had simply gone home when his shift was up and he hadn't realized I wanted to interview him. I'm not sure I buy that explanation, but we'll let the matter rest.

WHEN I STARTED WORKING AS A reporter, the station gave me a desk off in a far corner of the newsroom. It was the lousiest desk, since I was the youngest guy, but it had one advantage in that I sat across from Jack Kuenzie, who was then the senior reporter. He was whip smart, had a dry sense of humor, and possessed great institutional knowledge, having been at WIS since 1984 (when I was five). The news director, I gathered, had deliberately sat me there so I could learn from Kuenzie by osmosis. He could come back from a shoot and hammer out a story on a thirty-minute deadline—a complete old-school pro. Meanwhile, I was poring over every word, every sentence in my stories, while stressing out that I wasn't going to make my deadline. Jack would periodically chime in or offer a quip. I revered and respected him, but I never told him. You couldn't really talk to Jack like that back then; he wasn't into sentiment. I don't think he viewed me as anything close to an equal for a long time, but I believe I eventually earned his respect.

It took a while, though; early on, I had some rough going. In August 2002, when I'd been at the station only a little over a year, a big local story broke. A young guy had gone on a small-scale shooting spree over several days, and his latest attack had taken place late one night at a Texas Roadhouse restaurant in Columbia. One man had been killed so far. I was the early-morning reporter the next day, which meant that I was responsible for going out to cover any breaking news that happened between the hours of eight and eleven, before the real reporters showed up. Lo and behold, the call came in about the Texas Roadhouse killing and they sent me out to the crime scene. It was a big developing story with the shooter still at large—a test I wasn't ready for, though I did my best

I talked to a police official, trying to glean a few insights about the state of the investigation, but I didn't have a whole lot to go on. Still, I had to do a remote for the noon newscast, and I was barely prepared. I had rushed to the scene but nearly didn't make it in time: if I went live at 12:02, I had probably arrived at 11:57. I was shaky from the start, and once I ran through the few actual facts I had to report, I stopped talking for a moment. When I started speaking again, my mouth was moving faster than my brain. I tripped over my words, throwing in a bunch of ums and ahs. It was basically a word salad. Sure, part of the problem was how little time I had to prepare, but part of it was overconfidence. I had thought I could wing it, and in that moment, I learned that you can't wing it, especially in a breaking news situation. I learned a valuable lesson that day, but I needed Jack to help it sink in.

Sometimes—especially in local news, but this remains true for me even now, at NBC—a live segment will feel a little shaky in the moment, but then you go back and watch it and realize it was better than you initially thought. So when I got back to the station after the Texas Roadhouse remote, I was looking for some comfort, some solace. Basically, I was hoping for a veteran reporter to say, "Don't sweat it, kid. It wasn't so bad."

Jack was at his desk and I asked if he'd seen my report.

"Yeah, I caught it," he said flatly.

"What'd you think?" I asked. "It felt a little rocky. Was it as bad as it seemed?"

"No, no, no," Jack replied without missing a beat. "It was probably worse than it seemed." For a split second I thought—*hoped*—he was kidding, but he went on: "It was bad, really bad. Like, bad enough we were all standing around watching." I felt sick. But lesson learned.

The shooter, a kid named Quincy Allen, was arrested a few days later. It turned out he was a former student of my mom's. He was only six months younger than I was, and had ended up killing four people. Part of his motivation, he told police, was that he thought he had an opportunity to become a Mafia hit man, so he was practicing his prospective trade. Mom was not entirely stunned by the news. Quincy had struck her as troubled even at a very early age. He ended up pleading guilty to multiple crimes, including two murders. Since

2007, he's been on South Carolina's death row. In 2009 he and another inmate were accused of stabbing a corrections officer with a makeshift knife.

ONE OF THE BIGGEST EARLY STORIES I worked on at WIS was a riot that broke out at Lee Correctional Institution, a high-security state prison in Bishopville, South Carolina, about an hour from Columbia. This was in October 2003, when I was twenty-four. Five inmates using homemade knives had managed to take two corrections officers hostage, one of whom had been beaten and stabbed in the shoulder. He was in pretty bad shape—the authorities were worried he would be killed if the inmates' demands weren't met. One of those demands was to talk to a local news reporter.

I was already reporting from the scene with a satellite truck and a crew. I had developed a relationship with a fellow named Jon Ozmint, who at the time was the director of the South Carolina Department of Corrections. I called him on his cell phone to get his take on what was happening and find out how the authorities planned to respond. When he called me back, he asked if I'd be willing to go in and talk to the inmates and help defuse the situation. I probably should have been warier, more cautious, but I was twenty-four, I'd been at the station for only two years, and I was stoked. As a journalist, you long for access, even if that access requires you to walk into an active prison riot. *Absolutely, I'll go,* I told Ozmint. I'm not entirely sure why he asked me out of the slew of reporters who were outside the prison, but having dealt with me before, maybe he trusted me. It probably also helped that I'm black, since the lion's share of the inmates were black. Plus I was young. I wouldn't be at all surprised if Ozmint thought, *This kid doesn't know any better. He'll probably do anything to advance his career.*

I had to clear it with WIS, so I spoke to my news director, along with one of the main anchors and a company lawyer. There may have been one or two more people on the conference call. They were justifiably concerned about my safety, and they also wanted to make sure I wasn't being used as a pawn by the Department of Corrections. In the end, though, they left it up to me. By this point I'd grown a lot more apprehensive—in fact, I was downright scared—but I wanted to tell the story. I also believed, then and now, that if I didn't go in, the inmates were going to kill the officers, either deliberately or accidentally.

I got a five-minute briefing from a hostage negotiator who had been brought in by the Department of Corrections. He told me, "Don't make any promises. Do what you do professionally—listen. They want someone to talk to, with a microphone. So just keep your distance and listen." He also said, "You seem pretty relaxed right now. When you get in there, try and stay that way." In truth I wasn't relaxed one bit: he was misinterpreting my deer-in-the-headlights look. I didn't know what I didn't know, except that I was very much out of my depth.

The negotiator had already been inside to talk to the inmates, so he tried to prepare me for what I was going to see—"Just so you know," he said—but I was still shocked when a photographer and I were escorted in by two corrections officers. Even though much of the prison had been secured and was swarming with members of what looked like an extensive SWAT team, the scene was still bedlam. Men were screaming—so many and so loudly that you couldn't make out what they were saying. It was just an angry, frightening cacophony. They had set mattresses on fire, there was still smoke, the place was wrecked. I started thinking, *Maybe this wasn't such a great idea.*

The meeting took place in a common area on one of the cell-blocks, where the inmates had the corrections officers tied to chairs. The one officer had bled quite a bit from his stab wound. He had some kind of makeshift bandage and tourniquet, but he seemed a little out of it. Both officers were visibly nervous. The inmates were very angry, and we heard them out as they told stories about mistreatment they'd endured, including that they'd allegedly been beaten while shackled. I believed they had indeed been abused to some extent— and I've since spent enough time in prisons on other stories to be fairly certain that inmates don't riot unless they're fed up and desperate. The demands turned out to be pretty vague, though. It was what the negotiator had said: they mainly wanted somebody to talk to, to take them seriously. All told, the photographer and I were inside for no more than thirty minutes. Shortly after we left, it was over. The inmates released the officers and were taken into custody.

It was only after the fact that I realized just how much I'd taken on. If events had gone the other way, if one or both of the officers had been killed, I might arguably have been to blame, at least in part. The story could have been "Young reporter called in to defuse hostage standoff; correction officer ends up dead."

Ever since then, however, I've felt more comfortable doing prison stories. I truly believe that journalists have a special obligation to the weakest and most vulnerable among us. Often that means reporting on children, the elderly, the victimized, the impoverished, and the ill. But one group that is too often ignored is the incarcerated and formerly incarcerated. So any time a story idea crosses my desk about prison reform or a program that offers opportunities to reduce the rate of recidivism, I leap at it. Not long after the riot, I did a multi-part series for WIS on the state's prison system in order to try and educate people on what conditions were like for men and women behind bars. I've reported on wrongful convictions and rehabilitation programs. I visited San Quentin State Prison in California a couple of years ago to do a story on a program that teaches inmates computer coding. Some of the men were hoping to find jobs when they get out, but many others, those who were going to spend the rest of their lives inside, were learning coding as more of a hobby.

My interest in prisons is also due in part to the fact that my father started life in one. As well, when I think of Grandma Rene having been incarcerated at one point in her life, and when I then think of the woman she became—the loving, generous churchgoing woman *I* knew growing up—I find myself infuriated by the tendency in our society to throw people away, to write them off, to let a mistake they made early in their lives define them. Forgiveness has to be part of the equation.

To that very point, in 2020 we did a "Dads Got This!" segment on UPNEXT, a New York City program to help formerly incarcerated dads reconnect with their families. We focused on a man named Harry Glenn, who had been arrested on drug charges when he was in his late twenties and sent to prison for ten years. He had a daughter, Anastasia, who was two years old at the time. When he got out, she was nearly a teenager and living with an aunt. In prison he'd seen Anastasia on occasional visits, which had left him only with an overwhelming feeling "that I was letting someone down." UPNEXT, a six-week training and support program, helped him reestablish a relationship with his daughter. "What I've learned is that to be a father is to be present," he told me. The program also helped him find a permanent full-time job; eventually he was able to buy his first house. Anastasia, who was sixteen when we shot the segment, had just decided to move in with her dad.

"It's very important that society give people another chance. Who doesn't make mistakes? The part that's important is that you learn from it and grow from it." That was Harry's fiancée, Rinata Bly, speaking. They have a young daughter, Kinsley, who's about the same age Anastasia was when Harry went to prison. "When Annie was little, I was in the street. I wasn't focused on home," Harry told me. "Now I can't wait till five to get there, because I know there's somebody like this little . . ."—he held his hand about a foot off the ground—"with a big ol' head of hair and she's knocking at the window like, 'Yo, Dad, what's up?' That's my joy right there. That's my reward."

Second chances. Thank God, Grandma Rene got one, too.

IN 2002, I WAS PROMOTED TO co-anchor of the weekend morning show, and the following year, I earned that role for the station's evening newscasts. I had been at WIS for two years, but being young, impatient, and overconfident, I felt like my career was moving too slowly. The truth is, I rose up through the ranks very quickly. I mean, I was twenty-three, I was anchoring my hometown newscast, and I was sitting next to a woman who I had watched religiously growing up: Susan Audé, an icon in South Carolina news. While she would remind me from time to time that she was old enough to be my mother, she could not have been a more gracious and kind colleague. She taught me the tricks of the trade when it comes to on-air delivery and editing scripts, but more important, she taught me how to carry myself in a newsroom, what newsroom leadership looks like. It's not enough to show up, read a teleprompter, and act the part. You have to take charge, put the scripts in your voice, ask the right questions of your producers. Thanks to Susan, I learned that words matter in news, and that a journalist's credibility is paramount. As an anchor, if you go on TV and say something misleading or demonstrably false, and you think it's not your fault because your producer wrote the words, it's still your fault. You're the last line of defense. You're carrying the credibility of the whole newsroom.

Susan, who was paraplegic and used a wheelchair—she had been injured in a car accident in college—led by example at WIS. But on some matters, she could be extremely direct: relationship advice, for example, which she enjoyed giving me, oftentimes unsolicited, throughout my early twenties. On set, during commercial breaks, she and I might talk about a date that I'd been on the evening before, or a date that was coming up, or just the general merits of someone I was dating. (You'd be surprised by how much gossiping goes on during commercial breaks on newscasts.) Susan had a very good sense of other women and would make suggestions about those she thought I should be associating with, and those she felt I should perhaps *not* be associating with. On both counts, I probably ought to have listened better.

When I first got to WIS, Susan had been anchoring the evening news with a guy named Steve Crocker, who is now the main anchor for the Fox affiliate in Birmingham, Alabama. (Susan retired in 2006.) After a while, it became obvious that the station was grooming me to take Steve's place, which was awkward. He's also black, and we were friendly, but here I was, at age twenty-three, being presented with an opportunity at his expense. I had no idea how to handle that dynamic. I was just young and dumb and eager to anchor.

Steve took me for a walk around the building one afternoon, not long before I took over his chair. It was a remarkably generous gesture on his part, and I don't think I fully appreciated in the moment just how unselfish it was. But Steve said something that's always stayed with me. It was a blisteringly hot day, and as we were walking, I confided in him that I knew I was young and inexperienced, and that I wasn't sure if I was ready professionally to be an anchor. Steve heard me out, then said, "Man, you will always be too something. You'll be too young. You'll be too old. You'll be too black. You will always be too something."

And it's true. That quote has proven itself true for me on a professional level time and time again over the course of my career. In fact, I wrote it down on a Post-it Note that I kept at my desk in Columbia, then in Washington, and now at the *Today* show. You'll always be too something, so don't let it stop you.

I ALSO HAD OCCASION AROUND THIS time to receive another of my dad's rare talking-tos. I had begun doing some light gambling, which—maybe predictably, given my family history—turned into heavier gambling. I was betting on football and basketball games, and between 2005 and 2006 I took three trips to Las Vegas with different groups of friends. All told, I was losing a lot more than I was winning. One day Pops was over at my house and my wagers came up in conversation. By that point, video poker had been banned and he was done with gambling. He was pretty stern with me, blunt and to the point as always, saying something like, "You've got to cut that out. It's not something you can do." He made it clear that he knew firsthand the damage and pain a gambling addiction can cause, and that he thought I was vulnerable to it. That was definitely an aha moment for me, like the dressing down I got freshman year in college. Shortly thereafter, I stopped betting on games. He had put the fear of spiraling out of control in me.

UNBEKNOWNST TO ME, EARLY IN MY career at WIS, a news director named Randy Covington sent a tape of my work to NBC News, in New York. The network was constantly on the lookout for potential anchors and correspondents to hire for the twelve stations it owned and operated in markets like New York, Los Angeles, Chicago, Dallas, and Miami. (WIS is an NBC affiliate, which means it licenses the network's programming but is independently owned.) I was invited to New York for several meetings at 30 Rockefeller Plaza, the NBC headquarters. The network decided to take me on, and we talked about which of their cities I could see myself living in, what the dynamics of their news teams were in those cities, and how I might fit in. Then, essentially, they shopped me around. I met with station managers in several of their cities, and one of them was WRC-TV, Channel 4, in Washington, D.C. The mating dance played out over several months, but I was ultimately hired to be WRC's new weekend anchor. And thank god for that. At one point I had flown to Chicago for meetings. The ground there was covered with two feet of snow and the temperature was twelve degrees. When I arrived at the station, I thought, *How are people living like this on a regular basis?* Chicago was not where this South Carolinian wanted to spend his winters.

WRC is where I met Jim Vance, on one of my first visits to the station. He had been the station's main news anchor since 1972, one of the first black men in that role in a major market. He had irritated some conservative viewers in the seventies with his Afro and muttonchops. In the eighties, he was upfront about the cocaine addiction that almost killed him. He became a prominent advocate of twelve-step programs, to the point that Mayor Marion Barry sought him out for help when Barry was trying to kick his own coke problem. By the time I got to the station, in 2008, Vance and his long-term co-anchor, Doreen Gentzler, led the city's top-rated newscast. He had left drugs behind, but he still smoked, drank, and cursed like a sailor. He was also on his third wife, drove a Harley-Davidson around town (and across the country once a year), and remained unafraid to speak his mind. He advocated for the Washington Redskins to change their name long before most people objected, especially fans in D.C. In 2013, he raised a good local ruckus with an on-air commentary at the end of a newscast in which he dismissed the name as "vulgar" and detailed its use as a slur in old Westerns. "Back in the day," he went on, "if you wanted to insult a black man, a Jew, an Irishman, and probably start a fight, you threw out certain words. You know what they are. They were, and they are, pejoratives of the first order, the *worst* order, specifically intended to injure. In my view, 'Redskins' was and is in that same category.... The name sucks. We need to get rid of it." That was Vance, as everyone called him, never Jim: straight and to the point. Blunt. Ballsy.

WRC was interested in me in part as a potential replacement for Vance, when he eventually retired. I was visiting the station and someone told me, "Hey, Vance needs to sniff you. He needs to make sure you're a decent guy." So I walked into his office and found him wearing a do-rag and an earring. This was a sixty-six-year-old man. He was also smoking, which by then had been banned indoors at workplaces pretty much all over America. I was thinking, *Who is this dude? I didn't know they still made guys like this.* There was a big signed photo on the wall behind his desk of Tommie Smith and John Carlos giving the Black Power salute while receiving their medals at the 1968 Olympics. He believed strongly in representation, and it was important to him that whoever replaced him look like him.

We talked for a minute or two. Then he said, "Hey, I got to go get ready for the show. How about we meet later at this place I know? Finish our conversation over steaks?"

I said, "All right, Mr. Vance. I'm looking forward to it."

Our dinner was set for an evening or two later, between his six and eleven newscasts. He wanted to meet at a steakhouse on M Street, in Northwest D.C. I drove over and was right on time, 7:30 P.M. sharp. I wanted to impress Mr. Vance, but for the life of me, I couldn't see anything that looked like a steakhouse at the address he'd given me; it looked more like some kind of nightclub. There were two big guys in front, and one of them asked me, "You Vance's guy?"

"Yes, sir," I said. "I'm here to meet Mr. Vance for steak."

"All right, come on in."

I walked inside, and quickly realized this was indeed not a conventional steakhouse. It was D.C.'s most famous strip club—Camelot. And there in the corner, not far from the main stage, was Jim Vance with a Cheshire cat grin. He greeted me with "I just wanted to see if you were the kind of guy that showed up and walked in and sat down." So I not only looked like him, but also, in his eyes, I wasn't afraid of him or of a strip club. Thus I passed the audition, and we eventually became good friends. He reminded me a lot of my father, in fact, in terms of his excesses and of his comfort in his own skin. During my years in D.C., I often went to him for advice, and I know he took a lot of pride in my success. After he died from lung cancer in 2017, I was honored to be invited to speak at his memorial service, which was held at the National Cathedral. A lot of famous faces were there—Bernard Shaw, Katie Couric, Willard Scott. But it was so quintessentially Vance that another of his eulogists was someone he'd met at a Narcotics Anonymous meeting years before.

I STARTED AT WRC IN AUGUST of 2008. Lindsay Czarniak, one of the station's sports anchors, was off in Beijing, as part of NBC's team covering that year's Olympics. I knew who she was, of course, and I knew she was smoking hot—I had looked her up on the station's website while doing my homework during the interview process—but we had never met.

So one Saturday early in my tenure, during the commercial break before sports, I was talking to the meteorologist, Steve Villanueva, who had just finished doing the weather. He had become a buddy of mine and I'm pretty sure we were talking about what bar we would hit that night after the show, just shooting the breeze, when the producer got in my ear and said, "All right, Craig. Sixty seconds," which meant sixty seconds until we came back from commercial break. A warning to get ready. That was also my cue to turn to the sports anchor, who would just be sitting down, to ask what the first story was going to be—"Hey, what are you starting with?"—so that when we got back from commercial, I could tee him or her up, say something like, "So, big game for the Redskins tomorrow." The idea is to be smooth and make it seem like we both know what we're doing.

To that point at my new job, I'd been working only with the station's male sports anchors. This night, Steve and I kept talking a bit too long, and the producer got in my ear again and said, "All right, thirty seconds. Stand by." What "stand by" really means is "Dude, get it together. We're about to be on TV." Somehow my timing ended up being totally off, so that by the time I turned to the sports anchor, we were already coming back on air. Moreover, I was expecting to see one of the guy anchors. But I turned and there was Lindsay. The best I could muster was to stammer, "Oh! Hey! Welcome back from China." And she replied, a bit more coolly, "Oh, hi. Welcome to Channel 4." That was our romcom "meet cute": we literally met on camera. Lindsay actually managed to pull the video for our rehearsal dinner.

That would come three years later, after a few ups and downs on the way to the altar. Initially I pursued her, and after a couple of months we started dating. We covered President Obama's inauguration together, in January 2009, stationed along the parade route on Pennsylvania Avenue NW, at Freedom Plaza. Her mother later said that's when she first realized there was a spark between the two of us, during our live shots together. As for my parents, since my dad is such a sports fan, when I brought home a sports anchor, that was an easy sell. But he had been nice to every woman I ever brought home to meet the family. The same went for Ryan's girlfriends—even on those occasions where we've each wondered, in hindsight, *What were we thinking?* Pops was hard to get to know, he was emotionally remote, but in a casual social setting he was perfectly friendly and often charming. Mom is more the "never met a stranger" sort, bonding with people quickly, except when she chooses not to, which was usually the case with our girlfriends. Mom tended to give the ones she didn't immediately adore a coldish (but never impolite) shoulder.

I had dated women of all races, but Lindsay was my first serious girlfriend who wasn't black, and she was also the first white girl I ever brought home. (The same was true in reverse for her.) That wasn't an issue for my parents, Pops especially; Lindsay could have been purple for all he cared. But I was anxious about introducing her to Grandma Florence, who had such a mistrust of white people. We were down in Columbia for a holiday, and I took Grandma aside and said, "Grandma, I just want to give you a heads-up about . . . want to prepare you for . . . think you ought to know . . ." I was dancing around the subject and she finally cut me off. "I know she's white," Grandma said. "I know, I know." And that was it.

Grandma and Lindsay ended up getting along swimmingly. Linds had all four of her grandparents alive at that point, and she has a great reverence for people who have been around long enough to see some stuff. Before she and I got married, we were down in Columbia for another holiday and we went to surprise Grandma at the eldercare center where she sometimes went for games and socializing. They were having a party, so we sat at Grandma's table. She had a great time showing Lindsay off to her friends. She liked to joke that Lindsay was her daughter-in-law, but she was jumping the gun a bit there.

So am I. Lindsay and I dated for six months or so, but at that point weren't sure that we were right for each other, so we broke up and both began seeing other people. Neither of us was happy in those relationships, though, so maybe nine months after we had split, I reached out to her one day and asked, "Do you want to meet for drinks after the newscast tonight? Just to catch up?" We did, and that was it. We've been together ever since. We were both in our thirties. We knew what we wanted and didn't want; what we liked and didn't like. I proposed in the spring of 2011 in Miami, when we were on a vacation, and we were married that October, in Washington. It was a hectic period: that summer we had moved to the New York area to start new jobs: Lindsay at ESPN and me at NBC and MSNBC.

It had been awkward at times, working together and being in a relationship. One night early on, Jim Vance and I had gone out after the eleven o'clock news and I revealed to him that I was dating Lindsay. "Oh, man! That's fantastic!" he said. He could not have been more supportive, more encouraging. But I was worried about the professional aspect of it. "You know, this is tricky," I said. "What if it doesn't work out? What about management?" Like Pops, Vance was blunt. "Screw management," he said. "If it's going to work, it's going to work." He was proud that Linds and I had met at the station, and during our courtship he was kind of a godfather figure for us.

At our wedding reception, Linds and I were at the table in the front, looking out at all of our assembled friends and family, and at one point we noticed Vance at a table holding court, more than a dozen folks standing around listening to him tell stories. I said,

"Linds, this guy is at *our* wedding stealing the show?" But that was classic Vance.

Another memorable moment at our wedding: Mom and Pops dancing together. That was a sight I'd never seen before.

BACK IN THE SUMMER OF 2009, I had convinced Mom to bring Grandma Florence to D.C. for a visit. Her health was in decline and it was difficult for her to travel; her diabetes had cost her one of her legs, and she would eventually lose both. But it was important to me for her to come up to D.C. When I was at WIS in Columbia, she could watch me on TV for upwards of two hours a day, and she did. She took great pride in me. So I wanted her to see how I was doing in D.C., where I was living—to get a sense of my new life. Also, I just wanted to see her. I knew she wasn't going to be on this earth too much longer, and I had spent so much time with her when I was younger that she always felt like a second mother to me. I just always enjoyed hanging out with her, especially at this stage in her life. Pardon my French, but she had run out of shits to give and would say whatever was on her mind. She was unfiltered in the best way.

Mom and I had planned the trip for a while. I had bought a two-bedroom apartment in a condominium building, so she and Grandma stayed with me and slept in the extra bedroom. It was the Fourth of July. We wanted to watch the fireworks, but with Grandma Florence in a wheelchair, a trip to the Mall amid all the crowds would have been difficult. Instead, we went to the roof of my building and watched from there. It was one of the most moving evenings in my life, watching the fireworks with the two of them. Grandma Florence was so proud of me, and that meant the world to me.

She died in December 2013, at the age of seventy-six. The loss is still very raw for me. She had become bedridden and was living with my parents, staying in my childhood bedroom, where she took her last breath. My MSNBC weekend show had been playing in the background. Mom called to tell me she had passed right after I went off the air. Lindsay was then pregnant with Del, who was born in March 2014. I so wish Grandma could have lived just a little bit longer so she could have met her great-grandson.

CHAPTER 5

DADS
(INCLUDING
OCCASIONALLY ME)
GOT THIS

Sometimes as a dad I get it right.

One afternoon not long ago, I was at home in my basement-turned-pandemic-TV-studio, working on this book, when I heard shrieks coming from the family room upstairs. I ran up and discovered Sibby, then three and a half, crying hysterically. Six-year-old Del had decided he would slap his little sister in the face because she had taken a flip-flop that belonged to him. That was his way of resolving the conflict. It wasn't the first time he'd hit his sister or pushed her, but he'd never slapped her in the face before. So he was crying, too; he realized how bad what he had done was. That's Del's default reaction when he's done something he knows is wrong. He produces this heaving sob, where he struggles to catch his breath.

It's effective. You feel bad for him. Like a lot of kids, Del sometimes has trouble expressing his feelings when emotions, especially anger, overwhelm him. And to be fair, his sister often gives him a reason to be angry.

Still, he needed a talking-to and a time-out. (Back when I was growing up, I would have received much worse.) Lindsay had come down from her office upstairs, and we spoke to Del about the importance of using his words, not his hands. This was what I call hard-core parenting—not the easy autopilot stuff like "Eat your broccoli" or "Stay out of the street." Once in a while I actually find myself coming up with great dad lines. They come to me out of the blue, as if from the muses of fatherhood. This time I said to my sweet son, who'd stopped sobbing as he was sitting in this leather chair in our living room, serving his time-out, "Del, how would you feel if I slapped you or if Mommy slapped you? How would you feel about that?"

He said, "I would feel so bad." He kept repeating it. "I would feel so bad."

"You know what, Del?" I said. "That's why we don't do it. That's why we don't use our hands to express ourselves."

He took that in while Lindsay looked at me with a surprised expression, like, *Where did that come from?* I will tell you, as a dad, it felt like a mic drop. I walked back downstairs to my office, wanting Del to simmer on that. But I also wanted to leave on a high note, and that's one thing working in television teaches you to recognize—a good exit line.

I WAS ESPECIALLY PROUD OF MY response because I often screw up those moments by either overreacting or underreacting. As a father, I'm definitely a work in progress. Like most of us, I'm always learning.

Ten-year-old me in 1989, sitting on the trunk of my dad's 1973 Pontiac LeMans. That car, which Pops was constantly working on, was such a big part of both our lives—and ultimately, when he let the car deteriorate, a symbolic casualty of his drinking.

A family portrait from around the same time: Mom; Pops; my younger brother, Ryan; and me.

The Wileys: My mother Betty Jo's childhood family in their home in Cayce, 1960. From left: My grandma Florence, Aunt Ella, Mom, and Grandpa Frank. It was Grandma who kept the family together in the face of Grandpa's abuse and neglect.

My father, Lawrence Melvin, in the Air Force, early 1970s. He and Mom were an off-and-on item in those days.

Pops and me on my first birthday, 1980.

My parents, Lawrence and Betty Jo Melvin, cutting the cake at their wedding reception, 1982. I was three; what I remember is the punch bowl.

My dad's mother, Surena Smith—Grandma Rene to me. Sunday dinners at her house were a family ritual.

Grandma Florence with Ryan and me, circa 1986. When I was little, no one could make me laugh like she could.

My older brother, Lawrence (left), and me, late 1980s. Lawrence lived with his grandparents on a farm about an hour and a half from our home, but Mom saw to it that we spent time together.

The New Life Baptist Church, in Cayce, where we worshiped with Mom's family every Sunday. That's Mom at the front of the church, in yellow, receiving a big embrace from me.

Me as a teenager, circa 1998, when I had finally escaped Mom's fashion dictates. That's a Tommy Hilfiger shirt I'm wearing, which I proudly bought with my own money. Someone had told me it was cool.

My graduation from Wofford College, 2001. From left: Ryan, Mom, me, and Pops. That day Pops told me he was proud of me—something he'd said from time to time, but for once I really felt it.

Another snapshot from graduation: Pops with his older brother, my uncle James, who took an early interest in my education. When I was in elementary school, he had incentivized getting good grades by paying me for As and Bs.

One more graduation shot: Me with my dad's older sister, Carrie Mae. She was like a second mother to Pops—and a formative influence on me.

Visiting Pops at the post office for a "Craig Cam" segment on my first broadcast job at my hometown station, WIS, in Columbia, circa 2002. When it came time to do the interview live on air, Pops disappeared.

With Jim Vance at WRC in Washington, D.C. He was one of the first black anchormen in a major market and a legendary figure in D.C. When I was interviewing at the station, in 2008, he arranged for us to have dinner—at a strip club, to see how I'd react.

Wedding day with Lindsay Czarniak, 2011. She had been a sports anchor at WRC, where we first met literally on camera.

Pops at our wedding with Jasmine, Ryan's daughter and the first grandchild in our family. During her illness, Pops would be a constant presence at the hospital.

Ryan and his wife, Zully, with their daughter, Jasmine, at least a year before she was diagnosed with a rare form of cancer.

Lawrence, Ryan, and me at Hilton Head, South Carolina, during our annual Melvin family summer getaway, 2017. Ryan is the comedian of the family. Lawrence was more buttoned-down, but he had his own sly, sometimes dark sense of humor.

From left: My nephew Jayden; Ryan's wife, Zully; Lawrence's wife, Angela; Lindsay; and Mom, Hilton Head, 2017.

With Lindsay, Sibby, and Del on the *Today* show plaza, 2017. I'm still figuring out what it means to be a good dad, but once in a while I feel like I get it right.

Sharing Maine lobsters with Al Roker on one of our first *Today* show "buddy trips." Off camera, I was scrambling to help find a rehab facility for Pops.

A trip to New York's American Museum of Natural History with Del and Pops. Post-recovery, Pops has been a devoted, active grandfather. "Who is that guy?" Ryan and I marveled on a recent family trip.

Before Del was born, TV and movies had to a large extent shaped my view of fatherhood, which was fairly romantic. Or maybe I should say that with my own father and grandfathers as negative role models, I had polarized ideas about how to be and not be a dad. On the aspirational side, when you grow up with Dr. Heathcliff Huxtable as your positive role model—notwithstanding what we now know about Bill Cosby—no father is ever going to rise to that level; there's no room on the pedestal for regular dads.

I used to see fatherhood as black and white, good and bad, but real life is mostly lived in gray areas, in reacting to curve balls and surprises. I tried to prepare before we had kids. I read a book or two about parenting, and Lindsay and I talked about the kind of dad that I wanted to be. I had set pretty high expectations for myself as a dad, aiming to join Dr. Huxtable atop that pedestal.

Of course, all your plans go out the window when your kids actually arrive.

I have an admittedly weird habit when I'm nervous: I file my nails with an emery board. So the weekend Lindsay was due to give birth to Del, I was filing away. I'm lucky I still have fingers. We were enduring a long, slow Sunday when she finally said, "I think I'm going to have the baby." Off we went to the hospital, where the doctors didn't think she was near enough and wanted to send us home. "No," Lindsay said, "I'm pretty sure we're going to have the baby *real soon*." But the doctors insisted, so we went home, and then more or less turned around. A few hours later, Del was born.

We had decided not to learn our baby's sex in advance, feeling that at this point in life, there are very few good surprises left. Thus I had two jobs in the delivery room: cut the umbilical cord and tell Lindsay if she'd given birth to a boy or a girl. It was the first time I'd ever been in a delivery room. Prison riots and crime scenes were one thing; this was something else. I didn't fully appreciate what was about to happen and soon realized I was in over my head. There was blood and screaming; it all moved so quickly. Suddenly Del was out, in the doctor's hands.

Lindsay was gasping. "What is it? What is it?"

I was like, "Oh, it's here!"

"What is the sex?"

"It's . . . ahhh . . ."

I know, I know: I've spent my career on live TV covering breaking news, but in this moment I froze. Finally the doctor took pity on me, or on Lindsay, and declared, "It's a boy."

"Yes!" I shouted, redundant but eager. "It's a boy! It's a boy!"

The truth is, you can barely tell if a kid is even human at first. I definitely wasn't prepared for what babies look like when they're fresh out of the womb.

Another thing that surprised me was how we left the hospital. I thought we'd have to take some tests, like when you apply for your driver's license. I kept thinking, *Shouldn't there be more people making us sign stuff or at least checking to make sure we know what we're doing?* Basically, they wave you out the door as long as you have a car seat. It's much harder to file your taxes.

We drove Del home in Lindsay's Ford F-150 pickup—she has some redneck in her, though she mostly grew up in the comfortable confines of Northern Virginia's suburbs. I was behind the wheel, driving slower than I've ever driven in my life; Pops and Carrie Mae would have been proud of me. When we got home, I carried the baby from the car to the house, and that was it: just the three of us.

Hello? Anyone? What now? All that stuff I thought about father-hood—is it even applicable? I guess we'll find out in eighteen years.

The stray bit of guidance we got at the hospital came from a nurse who said, "He'll tell you what he needs." We heard that several times. I kept thinking, *How's this blob going to tell us anything? He can't talk. He can't even point.* Little did I know Del would be quite good at letting us know what he needed, even without the gift of speech. Sibby, too, possessed that talent in abundance.

I'VE RELAXED SINCE THOSE EARLY DAYS, but even now, seven years into fatherhood, I still grapple with what it means to be a dad. I'm continually surprised by both the joys and the demands. To give one example, I didn't fully realize how much Del would look up to me, how much he would look to me, even at a young age, for guidance. I didn't understand the weight of that, for him as well as for me.

What makes someone a good dad? How do you judge the job you've done? Do you measure it by how happy your kids are when they grow up? Do you measure it by whether they go to college and become productive citizens, whatever that means? Do you measure it by the kind of relationship that you have with them, if they trust you and if you trust them? Do you measure it by simply getting through it? I don't know. Maybe all of the above.

I do know that being a dad requires a lot of patience—and unfortunately, I am a fairly impatient person. The football season is a particular challenge, since Lindsay now travels each weekend for her job with Fox Sports as a National Football League sideline reporter. For me, those two days of being a single dad are like running a 48-hour patience marathon. I've found it helps tremendously if I schedule the days: we go to church, we go to brunch, maybe then a playdate or a family hike. If I can keep Del and Sibby moving, I find that when night finally rolls around, I can get them down pretty easily. Then I pour myself a nice tall glass of bourbon and call it a day— it's a satisfying "I got this" feeling. I was offended one Sunday night when Lindsay returned home and started talking about giving the kids baths, and I said, "Oh no. They don't need a bath. I gave them one last night." She looked at me like I had three eyes.

"What? You gave them a bath? Both of them?"

My dander was up. "I am perfectly capable of bathing my own children. What kind of Neanderthal do you think I am?"

Linds wasn't impressed. "Okay, then, when was the *last* time you gave them a bath?"

Well, I thought, it had been a while. Maybe I was a little too quick to try and clamber on top of the pedestal.

ONE THING THAT'S GIVEN ME PERSPECTIVE is reporting the "Dads Got This!" series, which we launched on the *Today* show in the summer of 2019. The segments have definitely struck a chord with viewers, who now send us quite a few story ideas. It's snowballed, if you will, in a good way, which tells me there's a hunger in America for positive stories about fatherhood—for role models. The truth is, those of us working in television don't get to harness our platform for good as often as most of us would like, especially these days, with all our country's turmoil, conflict, and tribalism. So using the show to spotlight a group of people who don't typically get much attention and to be able to do it on a regular basis with "Dads Got This!" is something I find tremendously rewarding.

I've also found it very helpful as a father myself, as I try to figure out the role and muddle through as best I can. Talking to some of the dads we've profiled, dads who in some case are fathering under very difficult circumstances, dealing with loss or dealing with addiction, but who are otherwise not so different from me, has helped me realize that we're *all* muddling. None of us, fathers or mothers, are knocking it out of the park on every swing. The point is in the effort, the trying. The being there. Most of us are doing the best we can with what we have.

I have to confess that the "Dads Got This!" series wasn't my idea. It came up one day when I was talking over potential stories with our executive producer, Libby Leist (now a senior vice president at NBC News), and she said something like, *You know what lane isn't occupied right now? The fatherhood lane. There's no one here telling the story of dads—dads who are doing remarkable things under extraordinary circumstances. Good stories are being ignored.*

You'd think I would have jumped on that, but my initial response was: *Eh, I don't know. You really think our audience is going to care about a bunch of dad stuff?* I thought there was a good reason fatherhood doesn't get the same attention motherhood does: people simply aren't as interested. I was skeptical that a series of dad stories would cut through all the noise and distraction and connect with viewers—I know firsthand how difficult that is, because our show tries to do it every day.

My conflicted feelings toward my own dad might have affected my sense of what would make a great *Today* show segment. Maybe I had a subconscious bias against the idea; maybe I found the thought of exploring fatherhood in this way painful on some level. But my skepticism began to change when we started brainstorming ideas. *Okay,* I thought, *maybe this will work if we can introduce the audience to unique dads—dads going about fatherhood in atypical and creative ways, or dads who are confronted with unusual challenges.*

It soon became clear that we had an opportunity to tell some special stories. Any lingering hesitancy on my part vanished after we did the first installment in the series. The subject was "dance dads"— the male equivalent of dance moms, but without the psychodrama that reality shows like to portray or foster. These are simply fathers who go all out to support daughters (for the most part) who love competitive dance, whether that support means building props or sewing costumes or driving the girls to competitions. We focused on a dance studio called the Southern Strutt, in Irmo, South Carolina, fifteen minutes from Columbia. (That we were shooting so close to my hometown was purely a coincidence.) Southern Strutt has a large contingent of volunteer dads, a group the studio's owners have actively cultivated. From our perspective as TV producers, we saw an obvious hook in a bunch of average-looking middle-aged suburban dads going all in on stereotypically "girlie" activities. I interviewed one burly guy with heavily tattooed arms—a deputy sheriff and ex-Marine, no less—who let us film him sewing ribbons and bows for his daughters' costumes. "The fact that they love it," he told me, "makes me love it." His bows were excellent, too, and he swore he also had a gift for embroidery.

Another fairly macho dad, a former SWAT team member, told me that he'd only missed two competitions in the twelve years his lone daughter had been dancing with Southern Strutt. He joked that he never expected the names Ashley Edens and Mandy Moore—a producer and a choreographer, respectively, of *Dancing with the Stars*—would be as revered in his household as Peyton Manning's.

Our dance dads piece was a fun, lighthearted story, but it also had a deeper emotional undercurrent. Dustin Pollard, the ribbon-sewing deputy sheriff, talked about having to work night shifts so that often the only times he could see his daughters was in the afternoons when they were at Southern Strutt—which obviously resonated with me. Dustin also talked about his own childhood, how he and his father had bonded over baseball but his father hadn't paid much attention to his three sisters, a wrong he was determined to right with his own three daughters. "I mean, I love my wife," he said, "but my kids are my heart." He added, "I'm involved with everything they do. Whatever it is, I'm there. And I'm there because they love me being there."

I spoke to another dad, Antonio Williams, while he taught me how to do his daughter Lakeyn's makeup for a competition. (She was a good sport about it, but I'm afraid I left her looking like the Joker.) Antonio told me that he first started doing Lakeyn's hair and makeup when his wife was hospitalized with an illness. "She was like, 'Hey, if anything happens to me, you will have to do this.'" Antonio's wife recovered, but before she did, he had to take Lakeyn to a competition in Atlanta on his own—and after receiving only a cursory beauty tutorial. "I was like, 'Man, I'm not up to this.'" But it turned out he was—and now, he said, being a dance dad was "a way of life for me." He switched to part-time work to better accommodate his daughter's busy dance schedule. "This, for Lakeyn, is a gift," Antonio explained about her dancing skill. "I was almost brought to tears the first time I saw her dance. She had that serious face on and didn't mess up once. I was like, 'Wow, she *really* knows how to do this.' Her dedication and her passion and her drive for it—that's why her mom and I work so hard, so she can have everything she needs to dance and perform at her best."

Here was a group of fathers going the extra mile for their girls, meeting them where they needed to be met. These guys loved watching their daughters perform, but they didn't seem to care all that much about dance per se. I'm pretty confident that before Southern Strutt their lives had rarely if ever intersected with spangles and bows. Their commitment wasn't about the activity itself, which could have been dance or Little League or quoits—it was about their daughter's passion, about connecting *through* that passion.

Which, to be honest, is one of those dad things I've been struggling with myself. One example: Del is going through a big Pokémon phase right now. I know *nothing* about Pokémon—or at least I didn't until I read his Pokémon field guide so I could talk to him about his energy cards and the characters on the shows he watches so avidly. I wouldn't say I've become a Pokémon aficionado—the fact that *he* loves it hasn't quite made me love it—but again, the point is to connect. I know who Squirtle is, and that's meaningful to Del. (And I hope someday he appreciates my effort.)

Another "Dads Got This!" story that resonated with me was on fathers, many African American, who have been taking classes online and in person to learn how to do their daughters' hair. The piece focused on classes taught by Tieya Riggins, who owns a hairdressing shop called Natruelly Mee Studios in Rocky River, Ohio, a Cleveland suburb. T, as Tieya goes by, said she started the free lessons as a kind of public service for men she knows who are separated from their daughters' mothers. "They get their children over the summer, visiting. So they'll come to me and say, 'Hey, T, can you help me with my daughter's hair? I don't know what to do.' So I just try to step in and help." T tries to teach dads how to do a decent braid, not always successfully. "A lot of the girls come out looking like Pippi Longstocking," she said. More important, she hopes to foster a "special bond" between men and their daughters by encouraging them to engage in a gentle, interactive ritual not usually associated with fatherhood. She even said it's "fun"—which hasn't exactly been my experience, but anyway. . . .

The dads we interviewed agreed with T that brushing and combing and spritzing and braiding their daughter's hair is less a chore than a chance for quality time. Frank Whitfield, a father of three daughters, told me that in his view, doing his daughters' hair is not only a bonding opportunity but also a kind of down payment, a token of deeper commitment. "I'm going to be there for them through every hard time they have," he said. "It's important that they feel that love, that they feel that love and protection."

"My daughter is my world. Everything I do, I do for her," Ricardo Benson told me. Another of T's trainees, he is father to seven-year-old Colby. "When we do Colby's hair," Ricardo said, "we do it at night. It's just a time for us to really sit and talk. I want her to understand she can talk to me about anything, and sometimes, doing her hair, that's when I get things from her I don't hear during the day. She's more relaxed. She opens up a little bit more." Ricardo admitted his hair skills were still "shaky" and that he hoped to learn how to "stop hurting her and pulling her hair." But watching him meticulously brush out Colby's hair one evening, she was calm, unflinching, and stylish in pink sunglasses, I could sense the special bond between them, although when Ricardo asked whether she wanted braids or a twist, Colby—maybe wisely—requested "just a pony."

I found myself readily identifying with Ricardo, as I did with the dance dads, and not just because I sometimes get roped into doing Sibby's hair—which, by the way, usually ends up an unmitigated disaster when I'm holding the brush. I'm able to fake my way through a ponytail, but that's about it, and even getting her to sit still long enough for a pony is a challenge. I brush as gently as I can, but invariably, twenty or thirty seconds in, she starts crying, "Ouch! Ouch!" And that makes me feel bad, so I stop; it's clear that hair care is not going to be a bonding experience for Sibby and me. Fortunately, she likes to wear her mane of long curls "wild," as she says. She doesn't really allow me or her mother to do a whole lot with it—thank God.

My larger point about identifying with the dance dads and the hair dads is that, in part due to gender, I find I sometimes have to work harder to connect with Sibby than I do with Del. Case in point: Aside from Pokémon, Del loves football right now. So at 12:55, before the 1:00 games start, I can sit him down, turn on NFL Red-Zone, and we can watch together for seven hours straight—no ex-aggeration. All he ever asks at the beginning of a game is "Who are we pulling for, Daddy? Who's our team?" I tell him which team we like—we tend to root for teams with quarterbacks who look like us, and Del is a particular fan of Patrick Mahomes and Lamar Jackson—then we're off. It's like watching a game with a buddy, who (1) happens to be my son and (2) likes the teams I like (for now, any-way), so I never have to worry about him pulling for the Dallas Cow-boys. Watching football with Del also rekindles warm memories from my own childhood, of watching games with Pops.

Sibby, on the other hand, couldn't give two hoots about football. Her passions—as of this writing—include make-believe, imaginary friends, and Disney. I can't get her to watch more than three consecu-tive minutes of football, which is a particular problem on those week-ends when I'm a single dad. Sibby will run around and amuse herself while Del and I watch a game, maybe play with dolls for a bit, but at some point I have to pick up the slack and do an activity with her. It's a system I've worked out, like alternating time slots. One Sunday last fall, my activity with Sibby was painting with watercolors. I'd watch thirty minutes of football with Del, then paint for thirty minutes with Sibby, then hop back to the game. I'll confess I demurred when she asked me to put some color streaks in her hair; I left Sibby's salon treatment to our nanny, Gloria Arumugum, who spelled me later that afternoon. But as I've done with Del and Pokémon, I also try to stretch myself to connect with Sibby's interests. I've become quite conversant with Doc McStuffins, Anna and Elsa, and Moana.

Gender differences aside, my kids have very different personali-ties. Del wants to please. There's little more he wants in life than my approval, on things small and large, and if he feels like I'm criticizing

him for something, he'll bristle or sometimes verge on tears. Without question, if I tell him to do something, he will—most times. If
not, he's still persuadable; I can negotiate with him. Sibby is tough
and full of strong opinions. She's the kind of kid who at the age of
three started picking out her own clothes. When I seek her cooperation, she makes me work for it. She will oftentimes refuse to negotiate or compromise. Bribes work, but that's a heavy-duty tool you
can't pull out too many times.

Sibby is also fierce. Lindsay took her to the doctor for a flu shot
not long ago. The pediatrician bought her cooperation with a lollipop,
but basically, Sibby was a champ. She didn't cry. She even watched
the needle slide into her arm. And then, when she and Linds were
leaving the doctor's office, they walked off the elevator and saw two
other little girls with their mother, waiting to go up. Sibby walked
past, then looked over her shoulder and said to these two girls—who,
by the way, were big girls, a few years older than her—"I hope your
flu shot hurts."

She turned around and kept walking. The mother of the two
older girls looked mortified, like she couldn't believe our adorable
preschool-age daughter could have said something like that. To Sibby's credit, Lindsay told me that almost as soon as she turned away,
she realized she'd said something really mean and was tearful for
the next twenty minutes or so. That gave me comfort that we're not
raising a complete sociopath.

My biggest problem with Sibby is that she recently discovered
the concept of "fairness." Friday nights are Melvin family movie
nights, and for a long time I picked the movie; then Del occasionally got to pick. One recent Friday, out of the blue, Sibby piped up,
"Wait, Daddy, that's not fair. It's my turn!" I was like, *Who taught
you fairness? Where did you discover these wonderful things known*

as justice and equality? But she was right. As they get older, I've had to be more mindful about treating them equally.

I'VE WRITTEN A LOT ABOUT PASSIONS in this chapter, and "Dads Got This!" has become one of mine. It's not only that I'm proud of the segments as storytelling; I really believe we're opening people's eyes to the many different ways in which men can nurture their children. And when I write "opening people's eyes," I'm including myself in that number. For instance, there was the piece we did on an organization called the National At-Home Dad Network, which supports fathers who take on the role of primary caretaker. Even though 17 percent of stay-at-home parents are now men, there is still a lot of stigma attached to the role for fathers. A lot of people hear that a guy has chosen to give up a career in order to raise his kids and think, *Oh, he's a kept man,* or *He's a trust-fund baby,* or *He's just lazy.* Raising kids is hard enough, but stay-at-home dads then have to cope with the slights and obstacles that come with that kind of antiquated thinking. Many also feel isolated in a sea of stay-at-home moms or mostly female caretakers. "I felt like I was on an island," the president of the network, Jonathan Heisey-Grove, told me. "I was on my own. I didn't know there were other stay-at-home dads out there." Another member told me he discovered the group when he "literally Googled, 'I'm a frustrated stay-at-home-dad.'"

I have to admit that before I talked to these men, I shared some of the unthinking prejudices against stay-at-home dads. I should have known better. There was a period when Del was very young, when I was anchoring for MSNBC but not yet on the *Today* show, when my schedule allowed me to spend two full weekdays with him. I'd take him to the local library for toddler music classes or to the playground, and I'd look around and think, *Yikes, I'm the only dad here!*

I felt that isolation and it was eye-opening. And now that I can't spend that kind of time with Del and Sibby during the week, I miss it.

If there is a single lesson to be drawn from "Dads Got This!" it might be that parenting is not a top-down occupation, not completely. In many ways it's a relationship like any other. Who your kids are—what kinds of personalities and talents and challenges and passions and needs they have—will influence how you parent; in a sense, they raise you as well.

One good example of that are the men in an organization called Dragon Dads, which we did a segment on. These are fathers from conservative religious backgrounds who in some cases have left their churches while joining together to support their LGBTQ+ children, as well as one another. Co-founded by a man named Jake Abhau, who was active in his Mormon church in Raleigh, North Carolina, the group started in 2013. That was when Jake's son, Jon, who was then thirteen, came out to Jake and his wife, Meg, one morning after he had seen two men kissing the previous afternoon and realized that he, too, was gay. First he told his mother, then his dad. "My initial reaction was, I was frozen," Jake said. "I was shocked. Not that we hadn't seen it coming"—Jake and Meg had occasionally wondered whether Jon might be gay—"but we were still kind of surprised. I was scared." He had instant visions of Jon being bullied at school, slammed into lockers and ostracized.

"I looked at Jon," Jake continued, "and he couldn't look at me. It was a really awkward moment for me. All I knew was I had the same amount of love for him, or even more love, in my heart. But in my head, I'm thinking, *What's the right way to react?* So I said probably the silliest thing I ever said in my life." It involved Jake and Jon's shared hatred of tomatoes, and their ritual of eating a tomato together once a year to see if their tastes had changed. "So my mind went to the one thing we had in common, and I said, 'You know, Jon, some people like tomatoes and some people don't like tomatoes. There are all kinds of people in the world and we just love them for who they are. We don't care about what they like or don't like.' I even remember thinking, *What a weird thing to say.* But Jon kind of looked up at me and smiled at me and I knew we were still connected." (Weird? I don't think so. I'll confess: I think that even beats my mic drop moment.)

The main thing, Jake told me, was he knew "I needed to learn how to be a better father for my kid, to prepare for things that I didn't know might be coming." Part of that, Jake and Meg decided, was to embrace Jon's sexuality and to come out to their community together, as a family, which they did with a lengthy heartfelt post on Facebook. Many friends and neighbors welcomed them, but Jake said they experienced "backlash" from others and from their church, so the family eventually moved to a more supportive Mormon community in Arizona. As Jake said, "When you're coming from a conservative background, and you have a kid who's LGBT, at some level there are things in your community that you have to face and deal with."

Meanwhile, the family's Facebook post was widely shared and led to the formation of Dragon Dads, initially as a Facebook group. It began with just a few men but now has over a hundred members. The name derives from a line of Mormon scripture: "They fought for their lives, and for their wives, and for their children; therefore they exerted themselves and like dragons did they fight." The group has become a notable presence at Pride parades and other events.

I asked Jake what his son thought of his activism. "He thinks I'm gayer than he is," Jake said, laughing.

Dave Jensen, an evangelical Christian whose daughter Natalie is gay, is another Dragon Dad. He explained his evolution this way: "I was raised in a Christian church and I was taught that being gay was not God's way. I was all in. I was ignorant. I grew up in Seattle, in theater, and I would have told you that I didn't know a gay person. That's how unsafe of a person I was to talk to, to come out to." Fortunately, not long before Natalie came out, Dave and his wife began to have a "change of heart" about homosexuality, in part due to the issue of gay marriage, which they decided they supported, though they were afraid to voice it. "We even told ourselves that we'd be allies, but we wouldn't tell a soul. I don't know how much of an ally that is, but I feel blessed that our hearts were changing." When Natalie came out, Dave said, "We tried to the best of our abilities to be as level-headed and loving as possible." Natalie herself said that her mom and dad told her, "We have no idea what we're doing, but we love you a whole lot"—which, truth be told, could be a motto for most of us parents.

Still, Dave was unsure how best to support Natalie; in his community there were no role models for parenting an out gay child, no one he could talk to. "It was important to me to find a support group," Dave said. "I had no idea what the future held. My knee-jerk reaction was that my kid was looking at a lonely road moving forward. I was taught that even if she was gay, she wasn't allowed to *act* gay. I had no idea what a successful and thriving life looked like for a gay person." Certain subjects, he felt, were completely beyond him: "I'm a dad. I don't know how to talk about sex to my straight kids, and then it turns out I have gay kids?" Dragon Dads set up a meeting with members of a local LGBTQ+ organization "to talk with some of us dads about what they wished they would have known when they were kids, what they wished their parents would have told them." It was all good preparation for when the Jensens' son Cooper came out as well. "Dad just said, 'Okay,'" Cooper told me. "It was nice *not* to have a really intense conversation."

Dragon Dads also helped when Dave and his family, like the Abhaus, felt abandoned by their church. He told me, with a palpable sense of pain in his voice, "As we supported our LGBT kid, I felt a loss in my community, with my friends. Something changed. It was a struggle. I needed friends. I needed people who were in the same place in life as I was." Dragon Dads and affiliated groups have given men like Dave a new community—and a renewed sense of spiritual purpose. "We help other parents learn how to parent a gay, lesbian, trans child. We just try to be there for each other." He added, "Having other dads to talk to—I need that community, beyond a doubt, to grow. I need that community to know how to raise my kids."

When I interviewed Dave, he was preparing to march in a Pride parade in Salt Lake City with a group of twenty or so Dragon Dads, most in T-shirts made for the day that read: *Protect Trans Kids.* "Marching down that street and seeing all these people accepting those around them—there's a love in that group," Dave explained. "After my first Pride, I literally wanted to start carrying my sign around and walking down the center of the street everywhere I went. It just felt so good to be involved." What really felt good to him was the effect on his kids: "To be able to see my kids go and look at other adults who are happy, who are out. . . . I still see in my kids a little bit of maybe insecurity about being who they are, and the more I can get them around people who are confident in who they are, perhaps then they can accept that in themselves and start focusing on other aspects of their lives they want to focus on and grow in."

More than anything, he said, he wanted his son to be happy and comfortable in his own skin—which of course is what we all want for our kids. You don't want them to suffer. You don't want to see them bullied. You want to make their path as smooth as possible, but without spoiling them rotten—that, to me, is the challenge.

SOME OF OUR MOST MOVING AND inspiring "Dads Got This!" stories have focused on fathers coping with—often transformed by—tragedy. One man we profiled is Steven D'Achille, whose wife, Alexis, gave birth to their daughter, Adriana, in 2013 and then died by suicide five weeks later. Steven and Alexis had a happy marriage and her pregnancy had been an easy one—Steven described that period in their lives as a nine-month "celebration of this new life." But the delivery proved difficult: Adriana came more quickly than expected—no doctors were yet in the delivery room—and there was a complication.

"It was just myself and a nurse with Alexis," Steven told me. "I'm holding one leg, the nurse is holding another leg, and Adriana is coming, but the umbilical cord was wrapped multiple times around her neck, so she had no slack to come out. With me screaming and the nurse screaming, finally we were able to get another nurse to come in and cut the umbilical cord. But suddenly there were sirens and lights and doctors everywhere. It was just mayhem."

Adriana was okay; in 2019, when we did our story, she was a sunny, curious six-year-old. But for the first month of her life, until neurological tests could be completed, Alexis and Steven were left in doubt about her long-term health, with Alexis already traumatized by the birth and its aftermath. As Steven told me, struggling to keep his composure, "People need to understand the heaviness and the weight a new mom experiences with a traumatic birth like that. My wife really, really believed with every fiber of her being that her first act of motherhood was harming her daughter." According to Steven, Alexis changed: "There was nothing behind her eyes from that point forward." Difficulties in breastfeeding her baby increased her sense of guilt. She began hearing phantom voices and baby cries. She also stopped eating—to the point that, five and a half weeks after Adriana's birth, Alexis had lost so much weight she was now ten pounds below her pre-pregnancy weight.

Alexis's underlying problem was a severe case of postpartum depression that none of the seven hospitals and crisis centers the couple consulted were able to diagnose or treat. Mental health clinics said her issues were an OB/Gyn problem; OB/Gyns said the problem was emotional. Some dismissed her anguish as "baby blues"—a supposedly normal reaction Alexis would soon get past, as if it were a childhood "phase." Though she talked about harming herself, an emergency room psychiatrist told Steven that he needn't worry about his wife going through with a suicide attempt. Why? Because she was educated and pretty. "Girls like her would never do it in a sloppy way," the doctor explained. "There are only two ways women like her commit suicide—overdosing on pills or asphyxiating themselves in the garage with a vehicle. So just go home, take out the car keys, and get rid of any prescription medication. She'll be fine."

Alexis's despair grew so profound that at one point she suggested to Steven that they give Adriana up for adoption. "If we just give her away," Alexis said, finding some inner logic in desperation, "all the problems will be gone." Increasingly alarmed, Steven left messages with several psychiatrists in private practice. "First call back I got was two and a half months after her funeral," he said.

Steven's account of Alexis's last hours paints a vivid, heart-wrenching picture of what living with postpartum depression is like. In the early hours of an October morning, baby Adriana began crying. Steven went to give her a bottle. "I was in the nursery," Steven remembered. "She wouldn't sleep. The only way she would stop crying was if I would put on Coldplay and rocked her. So I remember it was about four in the morning and Alexis came into the room. She just looked at me from the doorway and said, 'How do you do it?

How are you so much better at this than me?' I said, 'I'm not doing anything. I'm just holding her. Coldplay's doing all the work.' But Alexis just thought she was so inadequate, and that anything I did was better than her.

"She came over to me and she just said, 'Will you just please come lay with me? Please put her down and come lay with me.' So that's what I did. She laid in bed, her back to me, and I said, 'Babe, promise me you're not going to do anything. Promise me.' And she said, 'I could never do that to you.' I just said, 'I don't know what I would do without you.' She said, 'I'm not going to do anything, I promise.' Then she looked over her right shoulder at me, and she just said, 'I love you.'

"That was the last thing she ever said. I woke up and it was like all the air in the house was stale. Nothing was moving. She wasn't in the bed, and I just knew something was wrong. The dog was barking. I could hear my daughter crying. So I got out of bed and started screaming, 'Alexis! Alexis!' I ran downstairs and I could see Adriana strapped to the changing table. I kept running through the house, screaming Alexis's name."

He eventually found her in the basement. Alexis had hung herself. Steven cut her down. Her heart was still beating and she was rushed to a hospital, where she would live on for a short while. It was at the hospital, even as Alexis was dying, that Steven found a new purpose amid his grief and anger. "I was physically sick, mentally sick, emotionally sick. Couldn't put a sentence together," he told me. "Our childhood priest showed up and he pulled me aside to talk to me. And it was the weirdest thing. As soon as we started talking, it was like electricity came into the room, and it was like this clarity, this calmness like I've never felt in my whole life, nothing even close to it, came over me. It was like my mind was as clear and sharp as it's ever been, and my emotion changed from 'poor Alexis, poor me, poor Adriana' to 'There's a huge problem here and it needs to be fixed, and this is going to be Alexis's legacy.' It was so obvious what needed to be done."

The ultimate result of Steven's determination was the Alexis Joy D'Achille Center for Perinatal Mental Health, a 7,300-square-foot facility that opened in 2018, at the West Penn Hospital in Pittsburgh. Steven was so focused on making this a reality that he raised the seed money at Alexis's funeral. The center is one of only a few facilities in the country devoted to postpartum depression, offering therapy for mothers and families as well as childcare and other support. "It's been *my* therapy," Steven told us. "It's been therapeutic for my daughter. It's been therapeutic for our family."

Alexis's legacy lives on in the families the center has helped preserve. We spoke to several women at the center who told me flat out they thought they too would have ended their lives without the help they'd received. One, Ashleigh Griffin, said, "I get to live my life because of Steven, because of his passion for helping moms get through what was a tragic event for him. Everything he's done has completely changed my life and my family."

The center has also helped Steven explain Adriana's mother's death to her and has given her a framework for understanding that loss: "It's not a secret why her mom's not here. But she's a small child who doesn't have her mom, and I just don't want her to ever have guilt. So we talk about the problems in the healthcare system and why we're fixing it. She's like, 'The system's broken and my daddy's fixing it and my mom is the mommy of all the moms. She's protecting the moms.'" There's a beautiful framed picture of Alexis hanging in the waiting room at the center, and when Adriana visits, she likes to kiss it. "She is so proud of her mom," Steven said. "She knows we're doing something that's really special and so important. I think hopefully one day she's going to be the biggest advocate anyone's ever seen. She's learning through this whole experience that when something is wrong, you don't have to accept it. You can speak up. You can change. It's an important lesson for children.

"I hope Adriana tells Alexis's story with pride," Steven concluded. "I hope she says it and her eyes are open and beaming with pride and she says, 'That's my mom, and my mom's the reason for this change.'"

THAT'S ANOTHER INSIGHT I'VE TAKEN FROM reporting "Dads Got This!" stories: being a father or mother isn't just about the bonds we develop with our own children. Parenting can also enlarge us as people and help us embrace not just our own children but also others who need love and guidance. Steven's story is a dramatic, life-altering example of that—for him, and for the women he's helped. But the commitment can be smaller, of course, and still be meaningful, like teaching Sunday school or becoming a scoutmaster or coaching your kid's soccer team. Or starting a girl's wrestling squad, when you have a daughter who loves the sport but you live in a state where schools don't offer wrestling teams for girls. That was the case with Ken Corcoran, another dad we profiled, who lives in upstate New York. He started Team Alpha in 2015, when his daughter, Makenna, was five and desperate to wrestle. He started with nine girls total, and now runs a club with fifty girls ranging in age from kindergartners to seniors in high school—and now including his older daughter, Kendall, thirteen, who eventually joined up. "I've got two blood daughters," Ken told us, "and fifty more in the club."

I do believe in the adage "It takes a village"—that was certainly the case for me growing up—but that requires willing villagers. I was lucky I had such loving and available grandmothers, uncles, aunts, teachers, and other mentors. Not everyone does. I wonder what my father's and grandfathers' lives might have been like if they had benefited from the kind of support I did.

ANOTHER POWERFUL STORY WE TOLD ABOUT a father finding purpose in reaching out to others centered on Kevin Simmers, a Maryland police officer whose daughter Brooke became addicted to opiates. Kevin had spent most of his law enforcement career as a strong believer in the war on drugs, going back to the 1980s, when the country was flooded with cocaine and he had begun his career as a military police officer in the Air Force. As a member of the Hagerstown Police Department, he had been assigned to a Drug Enforcement Administration task force. "I really believed I was doing God's work," Kevin told me when we profiled him for a "Dads Got This!" segment. "I felt like handcuffs and incarceration was the answer, that the way to tackle this epidemic is lock people up and get tougher sentences, tougher enforcement."

Kevin and Brooke had had a close bond when she was younger. They enjoyed watching sports together, and he delighted in her lively, irreverent sense of humor. But like a lot of kids, when Brooke became a teenager, she grew oppositional and defiant, and started running with the "wrong crowd," as Kevin put it. He and his wife, Dana, knew Brooke was drinking and smoking cigarettes and marijuana, but shortly after she earned her GED, in 2013, the same year she would have graduated from high school, her life took a bad turn. She had moved out of the house but called Kevin and said she wanted to meet and discuss a problem. "I was thinking, she's eighteen years old, maybe she's pregnant or something along those lines," Kevin said. He was wrong: she had become addicted to Percocet. "She told me her life was spinning out of control. She didn't know what to do.

She wanted to know if I would help her, because she looked up to me like I could fix anything. And honestly, at that point, I felt like I *could* fix this. I felt like if we just did a full court press and got her into treatment right away, we could tackle the problem." At the same time, he knew it would be a long struggle; as a cop, he had seen the worst of the opioid epidemic, witnessing fatal overdoses on a near-daily basis. "When Brooke told me she was hooked on pills, I felt like somebody just cut my heart out. I know what opioid addiction looks like. I knew it was not pretty. I knew it was not going to be easy to overcome it."

It was not even easy to get Brooke the immediate care she needed, given the shortage of spaces in inpatient treatment centers, not to mention insurance company roadblocks. Brooke eventually entered an outpatient program consisting of evening classes. It didn't take. Her addiction worsened, she couldn't hold a job, and she started using heroin, a cheaper alternative to Percocet. The next two years were a long, tortuous downward spiral. Brooke entered several inpatient treatment centers but was kicked out for violating rules—once for having some ibuprofen. She lived on the streets for a brief period. She tried to detox at home. Kevin found her comatose on her bedroom floor one night with a tourniquet around her arm; she was saved only by a dose of Narcan, a drug that can reverse an opiate overdose. She was in and out of halfway houses and did a four-month stint in jail, where she was enrolled in a substance abuse program.

Throughout, Kevin and Dana never gave up on their daughter, supporting her every way they knew how. Kevin even took a leave from work so he could focus on Brooke. She returned home after jail, and for two weeks seemed to be doing well, though she grew frustrated when she couldn't find work. One evening, after kissing Kevin good night and thanking him for standing by her, Brooke sneaked out and drove off. Kevin and Dana didn't realize she was gone until the next morning. "We tried calling her and texting her, and we weren't able to find her. Then we got a call from her sponsor, who said Brooke had called her early in the morning. It sounded like Brooke was really sick. Brooke had said she relapsed. Her sponsor tried to get her to come home, but Brooke said she couldn't. She thought she had already embarrassed me enough and disappointed me enough. She couldn't do that again. So Brooke drove to a nearby church and crawled in the back seat of her car. She died there from a heroin overdose." She was nineteen, still too young for a legal beer or glass of wine.

Kevin had long since abandoned his get-tough, lock-'em-up views of addiction: "I did a complete one-eighty. We say in this country that addiction is a disease, that it's a brain disorder. But we don't treat it like that. We still incarcerate people for it." During Brooke's jail sentence, when she was sober, Kevin had asked her what she wanted to do when she got out. "She said she was going to open her own rehab facility. She was going to call it Brooke's House, and it was going to be for women who were struggling with substance abuse disorder. So I told her that when she got out of jail, if she stayed sober for one year and if she kept taking her drug and alcohol classes, that I'd get her that house." Within a month of Brooke's death, Kevin and Dana committed themselves to making that dream a reality. In a process he likened to the climax of *It's a Wonderful Life,* the Simmerses' entire community came together to help, offering money, property, expertise. "People just came out of the woodwork," Kevin said. "There's no doubt about it: my wife and I made a big ask of our community, but our community responded overwhelmingly. Their hearts were touched."

Kevin retired from the police department in 2017 to focus on Brooke's House full time, and in February 2018, the facility opened its doors. It can house approximately fifteen women at a time, providing not only drug and alcohol treatment, but also mental health services and career training and counseling. Kevin has made Brooke's House his entire life. "I've never worked harder at anything," he told me. "I do this seven days a week, around the clock. Even when we go on vacation, we tell our story to anyone who will listen. The facility is obviously a great facility, but we obviously have to have money to keep this thing going. That's what I've devoted my life to: to helping women who are struggling."

The week we spoke, six women were "graduating" from Brooke's House. Having seen the dysfunction, despair, and sometimes even disdain that permeated many of the treatment programs his daughter had passed through, Kevin wanted his facility to radiate the same kind of paternal love and support that he had shown his daughter—and that he feels all addicts deserve. "Brooke would be extremely proud of the way we were treating ladies at our house with dignity and respect," he told me. "I see a little bit of my daughter in every one of them, and I'm really proud of what they're doing and the efforts they're putting forth." He added, "I talk to every lady in the house just like she was my daughter. I give them advice and speak from the heart. I love them like they're *all* my daughters."

Coincidentally, after we aired our "Dads Got This!" segment on Kevin and Brooke's House, I found out that Brooke's favorite expression, delivered with a smile to friends and family members, was "I got you."

IN 2020, DURING THE HEIGHT OF the pandemic, I interviewed a man named Rob Kenney, who lives in a suburb of Seattle. He had recently launched a YouTube channel called "Dad, How Do I?" on which he posts videos offering what he calls "Dadvice" on subjects like how to shave, how to check your car's oil, how to fix a toilet that won't stop running. Classic skills dads are expected to have and pass on to their kids. Rob launched his channel in the spring of 2020 with "How to Tie a Tie"—perhaps the most quintessential dad lore of all. By the end of the year, he had more than three million subscribers. The videos are as straightforward and unaffected as Rob is—just him in the bathroom or kitchen or driveway of his modest suburban home, talking directly to the camera, and explaining how to do something. He's calm, competent, maybe a little bland, but bland in a reassuring way; he's definitely not the kind of dad who's going to blow his stack if you don't immediately get the hang of building a level shelf. People have called Rob a "Mister Rogers for adults," and I think that's about right. The quiet strength and decency he projects—along with his facility with wrenches, pliers, and dipsticks—make him almost the archetypal dad who's "got this," so he was a natural for our series.

This was a story I instantly related to, having had a dad who admittedly taught me more than I ever wanted to know about sewers and old Pontiacs but never managed to show me how to tie a tie. Pops tried a couple of times, and it didn't go well: he'd get frustrated with me and just take the tie and tie it himself and give it back to me. He did not have a great deal of patience, at least with me, and as a result, I wore clip-ons longer than any kid ever should have.

Rob Kenney comes across as supportive and caring in his videos, even gentle, and that appealed to me. He told me that the "Dad, How Do I?" channel grew out of conversations he had with his twenty-seven-year-old daughter about what she called "adulting"— handling the various practical challenges grown-ups are supposed to have mastered. "I was talking to her all the time and she was asking for help navigating life," Rob said. "And then I thought, 'I wonder if other people could use this? What do people do who don't have a sounding board that they trust?' I was just hoping that in a friendly way I could show someone how to do something. I thought I'd have thirty or forty subscribers and just a few people would see it. I had no idea this thing would turn into what it's turned into." Rob laughed. "If I had known three million people would be watching, I might have paid attention to the background of some of my videos."

The fact that he didn't is part of what makes "Dad, How Do I?" so effective: the videos are about heart, not production values. If they were slicker, they wouldn't be, well, dad-like. For authenticity's sake, he even throws in dumb jokes. ("Today I'm going to show you how to use a stud finder. If you came here looking for help finding a boyfriend, that would be a different stud finder. Ha! Dad joke!")

The comments on the videos are proof of a widespread hunger out there for competent, bighearted father figures. A few samples:

"I'm crying. I needed to learn this like 15 years ago . . ."

"My dad died last week and my bathtub clogged and I sat crying for hours cause I couldn't figure out how to fix it . . . thank you so much. I'm still in my teenage years and still need to learn. Thank you for this channel."

"I never had a dad. I had a deadbeat sperm donor, and an abusive drug addict stepdad. I moved out at 17, and I've been living for two years on my own, and there's so much stuff like this that I have no clue how to do. Thank you so much."

"I'm trans and my dad doesn't want to teach how to be a 'man,' so thank you!"

"It breaks my heart a little," Rob said, regarding the responses to his channel. "There's just a lot of brokenness in the world. It can be overwhelming reading the comments." He had a harrowing childhood himself. His mother was an alcoholic and his parents split when he was twelve, leaving him and three other siblings who were still at home to more or less fend for themselves. "My dad got a restraining order against my mother and got custody of us, but he didn't want us," Rob told me. "He would load up the cabinets with groceries and then he'd be gone for a week because he'd met another woman. It was just the four of us kind of looking out for one another." On Rob's sister's ninth birthday, when he was fourteen, their father announced that he flat out didn't want to have kids anymore, telling Rob's adult siblings, "Either you guys are going to have to figure out where these kids are going, or I'm putting them in foster homes."

Rob ended up living with an older brother, which was hardly ideal, especially since the brother was a newlywed who lived in a small trailer home. Even then, Rob vowed he would be a different kind of dad than his father was—which, of course, is a sentiment I knew something about. Rob is indeed a different kind of father, to his daughter and to his son, who is also in his twenties. He has a strong marriage. But he feels uneasy with his new role as a father to millions. "I have a tough time processing it. People are reaching out to talk to me, and I don't feel worthy of being in that position. I'm thankful that I am. But I also just feel like, 'Man, I tried to do my best with my kids,' and I get a little overwhelmed thinking, *I hope I do this right.*"

He finds confidence in his Christian faith: "I think God wants me to show his love in a very small way. God's so much more loving than I am, you know? But in a very very small way, if I can just share the love of God, because he loves me, if I can pass that out to people and just be loving, I feel like that's what he wants me to do."

One last part of Rob's story spoke to me and to my relationship with my own dad. A few years before he died in 2015, Rob's father, who late in life had become a Christian himself, came to Rob and his other children asking for forgiveness. "He was a little bit of a shell of a man, of himself, so I felt like I was kind of looking through him when I was talking to him," Rob told me. "But, you know, I've been forgiven much, so of course I was going to forgive him. It wasn't really that hard for me. I can't speak on behalf of my siblings—I don't know what forgiveness looked like for them. But for me, it was pretty easy."

Those words have stayed with me, and I've tried to take them to heart: forgiveness has proven to be a big part of my own family's story. Unfortunately, the horrific losses that have informed some of our other "Dads Got This!" segments, like those of Steven D'Achille and Kevin Simmers, have also had parallels in the Melvin family—not only in the past, but in recent years, too, and affecting us in the most profound ways possible.

CHAPTER 6

BROTHERS

Unlike many of the men we've profiled on "Dads Got This!" I haven't thus far been forced to handle significant challenges as a father—for which I'm deeply grateful. Both my brothers, however, have faced tragedies that tested them to their limits as fathers and men, revealing fathomless depths of strength and courage that have left me more in awe of them than of any other men walking the earth. These tragedies also brought the three of us closer together, which isn't always the case for families. For us, it's maybe even more surprising, because in so many ways, growing up, we brothers led three separate and wildly different lives.

I was six and a half when Ryan was born, in December 1985. I was excited about the prospect of a little brother the way I would have been if we were getting a kitten or puppy. Once the novelty wore off, the age difference made our relationship a little tricky. I wasn't really able to relate to him when we were both younger. Until I was an older teenager, I oftentimes thought of him as a pest.

There was a part of me that was also a bit jealous of Ryan. He was able to do a lot of the things that I couldn't. For one, he's musical in a way I'm not, and ended up on the drum line in the high school band. He's also a natural athlete. I played basketball and baseball but wasn't much good at either. Ryan was great at both. At six-four, he ended up being taller than me, too. (I'm a mere six-one.) Probably the perfect encapsulation of our different gifts is that when I was in middle and high school I worked as the PA announcer for the Little League baseball games in which he starred.

Ryan has always been far funnier than me, too. He's legendary in our family for his impressions of all of us, the women and girls as well as the men and boys. He mimics the voices, nails the affects, the mannerisms. But he never does this in front of the family member he's impersonating, so when he reads this in print, I'm sure he's going to be a little peeved that the secret's out. I'm sure he does an impression of me that I've just never witnessed. Some of that sense of humor I think he got from our dad, though Pops doesn't do impressions. His jokes are more observational and rooted in family behavior. He's quick with the odd wisecrack, and my brother picked that up. I might say something mildly amusing once in a while, and it's usually in bounds, but Ryan is truly one of the funniest people I've ever known and could have killed during the nineties on *Def Comedy Jam*. Of all the things I've admired about my kid brother, his sense of humor is at the top of the list.

Ryan and I are also different in that outside the family, he tends to be quiet and somewhat shy. I don't think it was easy for him going to the same schools I did, having a lot of the same teachers, and constantly being compared to his outgoing, gregarious (sometimes to a fault) older brother. He definitely enjoys needling me. *The Cosby Show* went off the air in 1992, when he was six or seven, so he was more of a Martin Lawrence fan, which became a thing between us, debating the merits of Cosby versus Lawrence. For some strange reason, he also became a Dallas Cowboys fan, which I find intolerable.

The first time I thought, *Hey, the kid's kind of cool,* was during my sophomore year at Wofford, when I invited him to visit me at school for his spring break. He would have been thirteen or fourteen, and he fit right in. He was funny, my fraternity brothers enjoyed him, and I'm pretty sure he had his first beer with me during that week. NCAA Football for PlayStation was our go-to video game at school, and I thought I was pretty decent at it. I don't think Ryan had played it before, but like pretty much everything else, he was better at video games than I was, and within the first day or two he had mastered this one, too, and was beating me. My bruised ego notwithstanding, we had a blast together that week and bonded.

The drama surrounding our family also started to bring us closer around that time. Now that we were both older and more aware, we would occasionally have heart-to-hearts about Pops, conversations that ran along the lines of acknowledging, "Yeah, our dad's a drunk, and we've got to figure out how we can work around that." We would talk about managing expectations for Pops, for what we thought he was capable of—or not.

There were times where I took on more of a fatherly role with Ryan. We talked about sports, high school, college, girls he had dated or wanted to date. I helped him navigate the adult world, landing internships and things like that. I knew what it was like not to have a father who could guide me in that way, and I wanted Ryan to have every opportunity. In the way that I grew up seeking Mom's approval, Ryan often sought mine. A lot of that was natural, of course, for both of us, but our approval seeking was also fueled by Pops's emotional absence.

Our experiences with Pops were definitely not the same. It wasn't easy for me, but I do think I got some good years and good memories out of him. By the time Ryan was coming up, Pops had become so sick and withdrawn from our immediate family, from the extended family, from society at large, that Ryan received much less from him than I did. While I was away at college, Ryan was still at home for the worst years of the video poker addiction. That was another thing I helped Ryan out with: navigating his relationships with Mom and Pops. Those were sometimes turbulent waters, and I tried to be the best guide I could.

Ryan tells a story about the first time he realized Pops wasn't like most fathers we knew. One day while Ryan was in the first or second grade, he was waiting on Pops to pick him up from school. That was the usual arrangement, at least on certain days: Pops would pick up Ryan when Mom was at work. But this day he never showed up. He had gotten drunk and was either passed out or gambling at Tom's Party Shop. "That's when I knew," Ryan told me. In that era before cell phones, the teacher waited with him for what felt like hours to a six- or seven-year-old until either someone was able to reach Mom or she figured out what had happened and came to retrieve him.

RYAN NOW WORKS FOR THE South Carolina Department of Commerce. He helps to attract—or lure, depending on how you look at it—businesses to the state; he also tries to persuade businesses already in-state to expand. He and his wife, Zully, whose family is Ecuadorian, met when they were both at Winthrop University in South Carolina. She now works for Blue Cross Blue Shield. I met her not long after she and Ryan had started dating, and it was clear right off the bat that she was someone special. Young Melvin (as I call him) had never—and I mean *never*—introduced me to a girlfriend before. They visited me in Washington, D.C., and I quickly realized she'd be around for a while. In what turned out to be a bigger deal than it would be now, Zully ended up getting pregnant while they were still in college, and she had the baby, a girl, while Ryan finished his degree. The baby's name was Jasmine. She was born in the spring of 2010 and immediately shined bright as the light of our whole family, bringing us all together in a way we hadn't been united in a long time. She was strong, feisty, funny, individualistic. An old soul. And she made one heckuva flower girl for Lindsay and me in the fall of 2011.

Pops used to tease Ryan, "Man, that ain't none of your baby. You want to go get a DNA test?" It was an obvious joke: from birth, Jasmine looked just like her father.

I'll never forget the weekend in December 2012 when Ryan called me sometime in the wee hours between Saturday and Sunday. There was a panic in his voice that scared me. I'd never heard him sound like that before. I haven't heard him sound like that since. Now that I have children, I can understand that guttural fear and know where it was coming from: the very core of his being.

That weekend, he, Zully, and Jasmine were in the D.C. area visiting Zully's family. He told me that Jasmine had gotten sick and grown increasingly lethargic, to the point that she couldn't walk. They rushed her to an ER. The doctors thought she probably had a nasty virus or stomach bug, but they ran a bunch of tests and some scans. A doctor finally came out and informed Ryan and Zully, "She's got a tumor the size of an orange in her belly." When Ryan called, there wasn't yet a firm diagnosis, but he knew it was bad. So did I.

I was living in the New York area at the time, working as a weekend anchor for MSNBC. I called my boss and told her I wouldn't be able to make it in that Sunday, then flew down to Washington to be with Ryan and his family. The diagnosis turned out to be dire: Ewing sarcoma, an extremely rare soft tissue cancer that is especially deadly in young children.

She immediately began receiving chemotherapy and radiation at Children's National Hospital in Washington. She was there for nearly three months before returning home to Columbia, where she continued her treatments at the former Palmetto Health Children's Hospital as well as at the Medical University of South Carolina, about two hours away in Charleston. Lindsay and I visited as often as we could. Pink was my niece's favorite color, so we decided to make pink bracelets as a show of solidarity and support. They said TEAM MELVIN on one side and JASMINE STRONG on the other. The nurses and doctors started to wear them, as did friends and even strangers. When you would visit Jasmine in her hospital room, there would be all these people wearing the bracelets, so she would know that they were on her team. It was a symbol that ended up meaning a lot to her and even more to the rest of us. I still wear my JASMINE STRONG bracelet. A lot of us do.

Another thing that really buoyed Jasmine was the song "Call Me Maybe," by Carly Rae Jepsen. That earworm tune was huge on the charts while Jasmine was in the hospital, and she loved it. She would ask visitors to play it over and over for her.

Watching a toddler lose her signature curls to chemo treatments was hard to take. So was the fact that every time I saw her, I could tell she wasn't getting any better. Before I would walk into her hospital room, I would try to amp myself up and make sure that I was smiling and cheery and positive, but Jasmine herself was always in such great spirits, until near the very end, that it was almost impossible to be downbeat around her. Besides her hair, she lost her ability to walk, but my angel niece never lost her spirit. Never.

When she was being treated first in D.C., then back home in

South Carolina, you know who was a constant presence at the hospitals? Not always my mother—she was working. And not always Ryan, who had to keep working, too, which forced him to drive back and forth between D.C. and Columbia, and then between Columbia and Charleston, shouldering a load few fathers can bear. Zully took a leave from her job so she was with Jasmine nearly every day. But the other constant presence? Pops. That was a sight to behold: our dad in those hospitals day after day, hour after hour, drinking cup after cup of coffee and sneaking cigarettes when he could. In a testament to the willpower that got him through all those graveyard shifts, and that allowed him to quit gambling cold turkey when video poker was finally outlawed, he gave up beer during his hospital duty—if not entirely, then nearly so. He had taken a buyout at the post office and retired not long before, which turned out to be a blessing. Being available for Jasmine and for Ryan and Zully may have given Pops a sense of purpose he often lacked. He sometimes spent nights at the hospital.

The way he stepped up reminded me of how he had taken charge when I was little and Mom was in the hospital. That's one thing about Pops: he might have been unreliable for large parts of his life, but even before he got sober, in moments of crisis, when the chips were down, he'd be there for you. He'd done the same for Grandma Rene when she was in the hospital, and for Aunt Carrie Mae, who suffered a slow, agonizing death from breast cancer. In these kinds of situations, he offers what I call a ministry of presence. He doesn't necessarily talk your ear off. In fact, he usually just sits without saying much of anything at all—as demonstrated by our days under the LeMans's hood, he's comfortable in silence—but his simply being there is reassuring and calming. He's from the baby boom generation, but he sometimes radiates the strong, silent masculinity of an earlier era, and in crises the family taps into that, drawing comfort and strength from him.

JASMINE WAS DIAGNOSED IN DECEMBER, WHEN she was two and a half, and she died the following June, not long after her third birthday. The doctors had given her every possible treatment, but nothing had worked. Ryan felt helpless. I felt helpless. We all felt helpless together. Her loss was devastating to the whole family. It was the darkest time in our lives.

I'm grateful for my career, and I'm not one of those guys in the public eye who likes to trade on his name and status. I don't believe in that, but I do have one exception: matters of health. When Jasmine was diagnosed, I didn't have all the connections I do now, but someone in the front office at NBC News reached out and helped us get a good second opinion. It didn't make much of a difference and I've always felt bad about that, like if I'd only been a little older, a little further along in my career, I might have been able to call in a favor with some VIP and found a doctor with a cutting-edge treatment or a clinic with a miracle cure that could have saved her. I've even confessed this to Ryan. I know I'm torturing myself, but I can't let go of the thought.

When couples lose a child, it seems like the relationship usually goes one of two ways: either they drift apart or their bond becomes even tighter. For Ryan and Zully, fortunately, it was the latter. I do think Ryan's sense of humor has helped him heal. He and Zully ended up having two more children, both boys, Jax and Jayden. To endure the kind of loss Ryan did and remain the kind of fully engaged father that he was and is, is just remarkable. He and Zully have made sure the boys know about Jasmine, and as a family, they treasure her life and her memory.

In March 2020, in the early days of the pandemic, we held a family Skype celebration on what would have been Jasmine's tenth birthday. Ryan and Zully had placed some of her favorite things on a table, and there was a cake. Via Skype we all sang and danced to "Call Me Maybe." Jax and Jayden took part, and so did Del and Sibby. Sadly, they're old enough now to understand cancer and death, and we've explained to them that they have a cousin they were unable to meet who is now one of our angels in Heaven.

LAWRENCE, MY OLDER BROTHER, WASN'T AS much a part of our lives as I would have liked when we were kids. Some of that was due to the rocky dynamic between Pops and Lawrence's mother. But he and I saw each other a couple of times a year. He lived with his grandparents on a farm outside of Spartanburg, an hour-and-a-half drive from Columbia. I thought that was odd, since his mom was alive and lived in Columbia, but she had addiction issues as well as mental health challenges, so that's why Lawrence's grandparents reared him. They grew crops and raised livestock on nineteen acres, and he was expected to pitch in with the work on the farm—we couldn't have grown up under more different circumstances. He would stay with us for an occasional weekend, and I would visit him in the summers. I enjoyed my stays on the farm to a point, but I would also think that this wasn't the life for me. I was a city boy and he was a country boy, and I didn't enjoy being out there for long stretches.

It was my mom who was instrumental in making sure that Lawrence and I spent time together, that we had a relationship. She was more insistent on that than my father was. Beyond meeting his child-support obligations and helping out with clothing, school supplies, and other necessities, he didn't really take much emotional interest in Lawrence—or Little Lawrence, as he was known, to distinguish him from Pops. When I interviewed him, Pops told me Lawrence's mom had tried to get the child support in her name, but "I had it sent to her mama. That's where he was staying." Pops said he was fond of Lawrence's grandmother, whom we knew as Miss Addie. "I liked Miss Addie—Lawrence had a good grandmama—even though she was calling me once in a while when he was smaller, saying he needs this or he needs that, and I would take it up there the same week."

Mom, though, really made a point of taking Lawrence in like he was her son, and she did so from the time we were little, when whatever feelings she might have had about Pops's relationship with Lawrence's mom would still have been raw; it wasn't like she reached out only after years had passed and wounds had healed. In a sense, she really did fill two voids for Lawrence: his mother was an unreliable presence in his life, and Pops was Pops. Mom was like a surrogate parent two times over. When Lawrence got older, she would offer him encouragement and guidance regarding school, even helping him out with his college financial aid application. He started referring to her as Mom when his biological mom died in 2019.

Lawrence and I were both at Wofford together—he was two years ahead of me—but we didn't hang out as much as I had hoped we would. Part of that was on me, part of that was on him, and part of it was just a function of the different social circles we occupied. He majored in religion; I studied government but majored in drinking and partying. He spent little time on fraternity row, while I decided first semester of freshman year that Greek life was going to be a large part of my college experience. He was naturally quieter and more reserved than me, though he was still active on campus. He was part of student government and a leader of the Black Student Union, which I joined at his behest. He made it seem like there was no choice not to join if you were black, though I wasn't nearly as involved as he was.

He was also on the football team, though I saw him play only once or twice. I didn't really go inside the stadium for the games. I was outside in the parking lot with my fraternity brothers, drinking. And honestly, Wofford football back then didn't usually offer much to get excited about, unless you enjoyed a sloppy running game.

Probably our closest moment came when Lawrence ran for student body president and I was his campaign manager. As a freshman, I was not much help beyond putting up signs and going around with him as he gave his stump speech to different groups on campus. Unfortunately, we didn't do a whole lot to grow his base. He did well with black students and the campus religious group, but we lost. I worried that I had somehow failed him. I also worried that I had let him down by joining a fraternity—and a previously all-white one at that—since the Greek world was far from his comfort zone. I wrestled with religion, too, vis-à-vis Lawrence. Should I have been more observant? But he never beat me over the head with his faith; he never dragged me to church on Sundays. He really let me chart my own path at Wofford, sometimes to my detriment, as in the case of my harder-partying early years.

LAWRENCE WAS AN ENTREPRENEUR FROM A very early age, building a shoeshine stand on the farm and earning money shining his neighbors' shoes. He also used to preach sermons in his grandparents' yard. When I recited our pastor's sermons on Grandma Rene's porch after church, I was partly imitating Lawrence.

So maybe it wasn't surprising that Lawrence became a pastor himself, though his entrepreneurial side led him to a slightly more unusual "day job" as a funeral home operator. (He handled the arrangements for Jasmine.) I once asked him why he chose to work with death, and he replied, "It's recession-proof. People are always dying to get in." As you can tell, he's a practical guy—with a somewhat dry and dark sense of humor, which I think he, too, inherited from Pops. While he and Ryan have very different senses of humor, I see aspects of our dad in both.

It was in the years after college that Lawrence and I really bonded. When I was living in Columbia, I threw an engagement party at my house for him and his fiancée, Angela, who had been his high school sweetheart. He brought a church group for a tour of WIS, and Mom and I would from time to time drive up to his church and hear him preach. She took pride in him.

Lawrence and I never talked much about Pops and his issues, or about Lawrence's lack of a relationship with him. We just didn't have that kind of bond. But in a way that helped us: we were able to develop an adult relationship outside the context of Pops. It was a new dynamic, if you will. We both enjoyed it, and over time, he became the kind of older brother I wished I'd had growing up. Lawrence has always been a bit walled off emotionally, which might be another thing he inherited from our dad, but I'm sure the fact that he was essentially discarded by both of his parents also played a major role in that. Ryan and I don't necessarily wear our emotions on our sleeves, but we're far from walled off. We can be big blubberers, for example: when we cry, we *cry*. Lawrence, though—I've never seen him shed a tear. The upside is that he's very even keeled, much more matter-of-fact about things, even crises, than either of his brothers. Lawrence and I used to talk about his challenges being a pastor at a small Baptist church. A big part of the job is managing the congregation's personalities, and when people reach out to their pastor, it's not usually because they're having a good day. So many of Lawrence's days involved counseling people who were going through the darkest periods of their lives, often dealing with illness and loss—and then on top of that, his other job was running a funeral home. It takes a special kind of person to be surrounded by death and loss every day yet keep giving to others.

His life in so many ways was terribly unfair. When his mom, who he believed was likely bipolar, got older, he ended up caring for her until she died, following a sudden stroke in her yard. He had done the same for his grandparents. Then when he was finally clear of those responsibilities and he and Angela were happily married with two young children—boom, he learned in the fall of 2016 that he'd been stricken with stage IV colon cancer. At the time, medical protocols said people should have their first colonoscopies at the age of fifty, or forty-five if there's a family history of colon cancer. Lawrence was thirty-nine. We were all floored. (The American Cancer Society has since lowered the age for first colonoscopies to forty-five, and a growing body of research suggests that African Americans should begin screening at even younger ages.)

Lawrence had been losing weight without intending to, something like twenty pounds, and also experiencing an uncomfortable feeling of fullness in his abdomen, so he went to see his primary care physician. The doctor basically dismissed Lawrence's symptoms as stress related, maybe an ulcer or constipation. He suggested some dietary changes like more fiber and prescribed a laxative. The discomfort didn't subside, nor did the weight loss, so Lawrence went back a few weeks later, but his doctor was still dismissive. The third time, finally, the doctor said, "Well, you're in your late thirties and you have no family history of colon cancer, so it's not that, but let's rule it out anyway." So they gave Lawrence a CT scan and found a massive tumor in his colon.

A few days later, the doctors discovered not only that the tumor was cancerous, but also that it had spread to other parts of his body.

The oncologist recommended hospice care, meaning the odds were that Lawrence likely didn't have long to live. One of his doctors said that even with treatment, if he got six months, it would be a win. He called me up, not freaked out—Lawrence didn't do freaking out—but understandably worried. I had a colleague connect me with the MD Anderson Cancer Center in Houston, Texas, which is at the forefront of cancer treatment, in terms of cutting-edge technology and research, and Lawrence flew out for a second opinion. He saw Dr. Scott Kopetz, who also treated Beau Biden, the late son of President Joe Biden, and who recommended a course of chemotherapy for Lawrence. (On Judgment Day, Saint Peter will wave Dr. Kopetz through the gates without verifying anything.) Coincidentally, Lawrence had his first chemo the same weekend Sibby was born; the treatments at MD Anderson would ultimately buy him another four years. They were a crucial four years given that his daughter, Addie, was seven when he was diagnosed, and his son, Lawson, was four.

Having had a parent or other family member get colon cancer is a significant risk factor, and there *is* a history of colon cancer in our family: Grandma Rene had had the disease. Unfortunately, Lawrence and I discovered that only after his diagnosis—a sad function of our family's not talking about these sorts of things. The fact that it took three trips to the doctor for Lawrence to get a thorough work-up is also sadly indicative of the chasm between much of the healthcare in this country and what's available in the biggest cities and top hospitals.

After his diagnosis, Lawrence and I both became very involved with the Colorectal Cancer Alliance, working to increase awareness of the disease, especially of the rise in incidence in recent years and the necessity for screening and sharing family histories. Lawrence dedicated what energy he could to the cause over the last four years of his life. Early onset of colon cancer—defined as occurring before the age of forty-five—is an increasingly worrying issue, specifically for young black males, who are twice as likely to be afflicted as whites. Survival rates are also much worse for blacks: 54.9 percent versus 68.1 percent for whites.

At the *Today* show, we've done a number of stories on the disease, especially during National Colorectal Cancer Awareness Month, in March, when we've also painted the *Today* show plaza blue, the color of colorectal cancer awareness. No one wants to talk about his or her colon or rectum—you don't; I don't—but early detection is key and it's important to demystify the disease. Lawrence was brave enough to do a segment with me on his diagnosis, encouraging people to get checked out. I interviewed him sitting next to Angela in the pews of his church in Spartanburg. I mentioned on camera how surprising his diagnosis was, given his age but also the fact that he never smoked or drank or partied. Lawrence laughed: "I was like, 'Man, gosh! I *should* have been smoking and drinking and doing all that other stuff before I had this diagnosis.'"

He and I have also appeared together at the Colorectal Cancer Alliance's annual Blue Hope Bash fundraisers in Washington, D.C. In 2019, though, Lawrence's strength had ebbed to such an extent that he couldn't stay for the entire event, but at the last minute, on a whim and without checking with anyone else, I asked if he wanted to get onstage and say anything. He did, delivering a message of empowerment for patients: "Maybe your doctor says one thing, or an oncologist or a surgeon says one thing, you still have the last say in your healthcare. Yes, *you*." The audience started applauding and Lawrence continued: "So I'm going to encourage everyone . . . once you decide that you want to move forward, you are always a survivor." There was a huge burst of applause. I might have even heard an "amen" or two. The Baptist preacher still had it.

A COUPLE OF MONTHS BEFORE LAWRENCE died, in the fall of 2020, I received a text from Angela. The cancer had spread to his rib cage, making it difficult for him to breathe. He would spend the last months of his life in and out of hospitals, with all kinds of secondary complications. We would regularly talk and text with each other, and one night when we were on the phone, he just didn't look or sound like himself. I asked, "On a scale of one to ten, where's your pain?"

"Twelve," he replied.

Deep down, our family all knew Lawrence had a disease that would likely kill him, but after four years we sort of convinced ourselves, "You know what? Maybe he'll beat it." I think Lawrence had known for a while that this wouldn't be the case, and a few weeks before he died, when he decided he was done with the treatments, the colostomy bags, the draining tubes, the pain—all of it—he brought the rest of us around to the fact of his imminent death.

What finally brought him to that point was that there was so much blood in his stool that his blood count, his hemoglobin levels, had dropped dramatically, and he would become light-headed. One day at home he stood up to walk to the bathroom and blacked out. He said that he awakened with two big white guys pushing him out on a stretcher and thought to himself, *Oh, man, I'm not going out like this, am I?*

While he was in the hospital, he told me he had signed a Do Not Resuscitate order. For a second, I wanted to question him—*What? Are you sure?*—but then it clicked: this was his way of telling me that he had made peace with his coming death, and that he wanted me and the rest of the family to make peace with it as well. Lawrence can be pretty self-contained, even a bit detached, and he wasn't always candid about his treatments and symptoms—he even kept some of that from Angela—so this admission was a big deal. I said something like, "So you've decided this is it?" And he said, "Yeah, I want to go at home." Then he added, reminding me that he was a funeral home operator, "It's a lot cheaper to die at home than it is in the hospital." That was such a Lawrence thing to say: practical, with that dash of dark humor. He also told me that he wasn't scared, that he had no fears about what awaited him on the other side. That was due in no small part to his faith, not to mention his having seen death up close for as long as he had, which gave him a unique perspective.

Lawrence and I also had some heart-to-heart conversations about his kids, Addie (named after her great-grandmother) and Lawson. His role as their father weighed on him for obvious reasons, but he also regretted that his illness had kept him from being as present a dad as he wanted to be. Even before his health really deteriorated, he was flying back and forth to MD Anderson once or twice a month for treatment, so he was gone a lot. And he wasn't always capable, physically, of parenting young children. He knew he was not going to be able to see and enjoy the milestones in their lives, and that was hard for him, of course. He asked me to look out for Addie and Lawson. I promised him that I would.

Lindsay and I flew down to South Carolina to say our goodbyes on the day he was released from the hospital. We arrived at his home just a few minutes after an ambulance had dropped him off. He was in a hospital bed in his and Angela's bedroom, next to a supplemental oxygen machine. We talked about his business affairs, and he wanted to make sure I knew where certain papers were. He had made all the arrangements for his funeral. The suit he wanted to be buried in was hanging in his closet, the shoes stored in his garage. He planned the service, to be led by a buddy of his from divinity school. Angela later told me that she had asked him what color clothes he wanted his mourners dressed in. "Black, baby," he said.

I read him an early draft of this chapter, just to make sure he was okay with it. I broke down sobbing several times as I tried to read. "It's okay," he told me over and over. "It's okay."

He was dying and he was comforting me. That was Lawrence. "You remember things well," he said—a compliment that meant the world to me. A kind of gift.

Ryan and Pops came over, which was nice; there haven't been all that many times when the four of us have been together. We mostly talked nonsense, sports or things we'd seen on TV, for the better part of four hours, with *The Cosby Show* on in the background—comfort food. The point for all of us was just being there for Lawrence, and for one another. Pops was doing his "ministry of presence" thing.

We swapped some stories about Lawrence's mom, who we always knew as Joan Meadows, but Lawrence said, "You know her name was really Joanne?" I was like, "Joanne? Since when?" He said, "After she died, I was trying to get her affairs in order, and I had a hard time finding records of things, and the lawyer told me I should look up different versions of the name. Lo and behold, there it was: Joanne Meadows."

I asked, "Why did she change her name?" Lawrence said, "She didn't, really. She just decided to call herself Joan, so everyone else did." Maybe she felt one syllable was more efficient than two.

The funny thing was, Pops's phone kept ringing. He and Mom had been in the hospital themselves for five days only a week earlier. Ryan had gone over to their house one afternoon and discovered that they were both having a hard time breathing and that Pops was disoriented. Ryan feared they both had Covid-19, but it turned out their condition was "only" bacterial pneumonia. The silver lining was that being hospitalized for the first time in his life finally got Pops to quit smoking. He did it cold turkey—that willpower again. Anyway, after that scare, we had bought him an up-to-date iPhone because it had been so hard to communicate with him via whatever dinosaur model he'd had before. For whatever reason, he now decided that he was going to be one of the last cellphone users in this country to keep their ringer on at all times. There are only five or six people who might ever call him, and that afternoon three of those people were there with him in Lawrence's bedroom. A fourth, Mom, knew where he was and what he was doing and knew not to bother him, but for some reason the other two possible callers felt they needed to talk to him that afternoon. So every twenty minutes or so that damn phone went off, and loudly. Pops had it set at something like 80 decibels.

We'd be sitting there enjoying our intimacy and fellowship when all of sudden, *beep beep beep*, and Pops would start fumbling with his phone. "Oh, is that . . . Oh, it's Mr. Johnny!" He'd put the phone down without answering, but by the fifth or sixth time, I grumbled, "Pops, give me the damn phone and I'll just tell Mr. Johnny you're not available right now."

"Oh no, don't worry. I've been sending him to voice mail."

We groaned. "You don't have voice mail set up!" Ryan told him. "That's why Mr. Johnny keeps goddamn calling." Dad and that iPhone were like something out of an *SNL* sketch.

Pops started giving Ryan a hard time about some trivial failing, and I said, "You know, you're going to have to go easy on Ryan now considering he literally saved your and Mom's lives." Then I made a joke about not wanting to have to plan his and Mom's funerals at the same time, which reminded Pops of a story about Joe Visconti, his old friend from across the street: "Joe some years ago had to fly out to

Arizona when both of his parents were really sick at the same time. His mother died one day, and his father died two or three days after. I said, 'Joe, how did you feel about that, losing two parents in three days?' Joe said, 'Man, I got to be honest with you, it was a blessing I was able to put them both in the ground at the same time. I only had to go to Arizona once. That trip is brutal.'" We all laughed. It might sound odd, but Pops telling that story on Lawrence's deathbed was a perfect summation of both their senses of humor.

Even before Pops stopped drinking, he and Lawrence had had started to repair their relationship—build it, really, for the first time—but Pops's getting sober definitely accelerated the process. I'm grateful that they had those two years between his recovery and Lawrence's death. Pops reached out to Lawrence's whole family and has a better relationship with Addie and Lawson than he ever did with Lawrence, back in the day. Lawrence started regularly referring to him as "Dad," which he hadn't always done.

THAT EVENING, AFTER LINDSAY AND I had left, Lawrence and Angela had a conversation with Addie and Lawson, explaining to them as lovingly as they could, that Daddy wasn't going to get better.

He died peacefully on the morning of December 9, 2020. Because of the pandemic, the service he planned was small—just close family, no friends. Lawrence to the last, he also wrote his own obituary. He had asked me to speak on behalf of the family at the service, but after his death I found out that he had two specific requests. He asked that I not exceed five minutes and that I not cry during my talk. I held myself together surprisingly well, though I did run a bit long. I don't feel bad about that.

CHAPTER 7

"WHO *IS* THIS GUY?"

To fix a problem you first have to acknowledge it, then understand it, but I'm not sure when I became acutely, consciously aware that my father's drinking was a serious issue—that he was, as I eventually came to understand, a textbook alcoholic. There certainly wasn't an aha moment for me, like there was for Ryan the time Pops failed to pick him up from school. It was more like a slowly dawning realization, starting around the time I entered middle school and continuing on through high school. I don't know if he actually started drinking more in those years or if I just became more conscious of it. I knew he had always enjoyed his beer, but at some point I noticed he was putting away more than just one or two every day.

There was an incident while I was in elementary school that, in hindsight, feels like a turning point. He was driving home one day on a main thoroughfare near our house when he swerved off the road and ran into a woman's yard, plowing into a couple of her bushes. He was presumably drunk, and in an attempt to get the woman to not call the cops, he managed to negotiate an arrangement in which he agreed to replant her bushes. Of course, I got roped into going over with him to do the work one Saturday morning.

As I got older, it became a given that by the end of every day he was going to be three sheets to the wind. His speech would slur. There was the occasional throwing up on himself in bed or in the bathroom. Our house eventually became littered with empty beer cans—you could gauge how much he'd had by how many empties were lying around.

It became obvious. Undeniable. *Pops was a drunk.* It wasn't a secret, not from us and not from the rest of the family. During the video poker years, if he was coming back from Tom's, he would be trashed. Working the third shift was also a recipe for disaster. He'd come home, he'd sleep, he'd drink, he'd go back to work. That became the routine. At some point, he started drinking at work, too, which we found out about only after he was in rehab. On his breaks he would drive over to a corner store down the street from the post office, pick up a tallboy or two, sit in his car and drink, puff on a few cancer sticks, then finish his shift. It's really remarkable that he was as functional as he was, that as sick as he was, he was able to hold down that job for nearly four decades.

The more Pops drank, the more isolated he became—a cycle that grew worse and worse over the years. He withdrew from our extended family, and then he withdrew from Mom, Ryan, and me. There came a point when I was in college where he was just inhabiting the house, barely interacting with anyone. He didn't really talk to us, and we didn't really talk to him unless we needed something.

There were outside factors adding to his problem. Grandma Rene's death had been a huge blow to him. Then, in 2000, while I was in college, Aunt Carrie Mae died of breast cancer. Fifteen years older than Pops, she had been a second mother to him growing up, really helping to rear him. In turn, when he was a teenager, he became something of a big brother or even a pseudo father figure to Carrie Mae's three boys—sort of like Uncle Pop had been for me—after she and her husband became estranged. It would be exaggerating to say he went off the rails when his mother died, but he certainly wasn't the same, and he was even less the same after Carrie Mae died. Her funeral was the second time I ever saw Pops cry, after Grandma Rene's service. His drinking seemed to grow with his grief.

Aside from Grandma Rene, Carrie Mae had been the only person he would really listen to or take counsel from; maybe she was the only person he really trusted. Even when I was a little kid, I was aware he had a special relationship with her; he always toed the line when she was around. She was a nurse and was well aware that he had a drinking problem. As it grew worse, she confronted him several times, and at one point, I later learned, she convinced him to get help. He went to some kind of outpatient class, maybe an AA meeting or two, but it didn't stick. Once Carrie Mae died, there was no one who could really get through to him. Mom certainly couldn't.

She and Pops were back in a cold war phase, even colder than previous go-rounds. Now that I was an adult, Mom and I had several very frank conversations—you could probably characterize a few of them as interventions on my part—in which I said to her, "He's miserable. You're miserable. Neither of you brings out the best in the other. I get why you stayed together while Ryan and I were younger. And two incomes are better than one. I get that. But now you really aren't doing anyone a service by just being miserable together." I told her I wanted her to be happy and that I thought she would be if she divorced him. I never got into it quite so deeply with Pops, but I did ask him once or twice, "Why don't you just leave?" I told him I thought he should go back and live in Cayce, in Grandma Rene's old house. I thought he'd be more content there.

Mom did consider leaving him several times. When I'd talk to her about it, she'd say, "I know, I know. You're right." At one point she rented a storage unit, in preparation for moving out. But she never did. When Grandma Florence was sick, but before she moved in with my parents, Mom would sometimes go stay with her for days or weeks at a time. That was as close as she got to living apart from Pops. Mom has told me that she doesn't really believe in divorce, and I think that's guided a lot of her ultimate refusal to walk away from her marriage. She once said, "We don't do *divorced*."

IT WASN'T JUST A FAMILY PROBLEM: Pops had become more socially isolated, too. A lot of his old drinking buddies in Cayce had died or drifted away, and working the third shift, he didn't have a lot of opportunities to make new friends, since most people socialize in the evenings. It wasn't like he and Mom could meet another couple for a movie or have someone over for dinner. As time went by, he became an increasingly mean drunk, sometimes saying really harsh things that would hurt and alienate people—the kinds of things he never would have said when he was sober.

He had enjoyed the fellowship at the post office, but even that soured as time went on. I watched all this happen. It pained me as much as it saddened me, but it also made me angry. I'm not Lawrence, but I do tend to keep my emotions on a pretty even keel; in that way I'm not unlike Pops. But there was an episode in my late twenties when we were arguing and my frustration, if not rage, boiled over. I really let him have it. "Pops, if you were to drop dead tomorrow, who would speak at your funeral? Who's going to get up and say something nice about the life that you lived? Who? Give me *one* damn person." He couldn't answer me. It was a sad, hurtful moment for both of us, and I've regretted calling him out like that ever since. But it was true: there was no one in our world he hadn't pushed away or disappointed.

AFTER CARRIE MAE'S DEATH, WHILE I was still in college, we staged a sort of impromptu intervention in our den in Columbia. My mother was there, along with Uncle James and my cousin Kevin, one of Carrie Mae's three sons whom Pops had helped father.

We didn't know what we were doing. We just basically ganged up on Pops and told him that he was a drunk and that we wanted him to get his life together. We had a therapist lined up that we wanted him to see, but we weren't trying to get him into rehab or even to start up with AA. We didn't have much in the way of an objective beyond just wanting him to do better.

I had set it in motion. There hadn't been any particular incident or crisis involving his drinking—nothing cataclysmic. I just felt sorry for him and wanted to try to help him improve his lot in life. I thought that if I could get the family together to express our love for him collectively, he would have to respond and act. So I called Uncle James and Kevin, and asked them to come over when I knew he would be home. He was walking through the house and I stopped him and said, "Hey, Pops, I want to talk to you about something." I led him into the den where everyone was. He sat down on the floor and we all peppered him with our thoughts. I'm sure he felt like we were haranguing him, because quite frankly we were. It probably didn't help that because he was on the floor, leaning against a door, we were literally talking down to him. Our message was basically: We want the old Lawrence Melvin back, the funny guy who used to bowl and hang out and shoot baskets with his kids and work on the car. We want that guy back, and here's what you've been doing to him for the last couple of years. We're really upset, but we love you.

Even at the time, I suspected this wasn't going to work. While we were talking, I looked down at him and thought, *This guy is not taking us seriously. He's humoring us so we'll leave him alone.* Which wasn't quite right. Pops knew he had a problem; in fact he was honest enough not to deny it when people called him on it. My father has been a lot of things, but never a liar. He promised us that he would cut back on the drinking. He had done that before, too, but he wasn't capable of stopping and we hadn't yet figured out how best to help him.

IT WAS WHEN I WAS IN my early twenties, after I started my career in journalism and became more familiar with a wider world, that I began to understand that Pops was sick. It wasn't that he *wanted* to be isolated. It wasn't that he *chose* more or less to quit on his family, on life. He had an illness—alcoholism. And moreover, on top of that illness, he had a whole host of other issues. He was likely clinically depressed. He suffered from an inferiority complex. He had a complicated relationship with my mother, who didn't always make him feel good about himself, directly and indirectly. At some point after our failed intervention, Uncle James tried to have a man-to-man talk with Pops about his drinking, but where he'd listened to Carrie Mae, he was having none of it from his brother. Nearly all of my dad's relationships were rife with complexity, jealousy, and resentment. It was like he was shipwrecked, alone on an island.

After I started working at WIS, I began seeing a therapist. (I'm a firm believer in therapy and have always believed in talking out one's issues with a professional.) A lot of the problems this therapist and I were talking about ultimately went back to Pops and our relationship. One day she said, "You know what? We should get your dad in here for a family counseling session. You should say some of the things you've been telling me to him." I responded, "Well, okay . . . maybe that's a good idea?" I was skeptical.

But I did it. I asked Pops to come in with me and he said yes. I was stunned that he agreed. So we sat in the therapist's office and I started laying it all out there for him. I remember the session as my having almost a diarrhea of the mouth, if you will. I went on for ten straight minutes without interruption, maybe even longer, talking about how disappointed I was in him and how I felt that he was wasting his life. I also said I loved him and wished I could forgive him and wanted him to get help and . . . I just went on and on and on. My life had gotten to a point where I needed almost desperately to unload everything I'd built up over the years. So much of the weight and baggage I carried around was related to him, and I needed him to know that. I kept telling him that I wanted him to get better—not just for me, but for his own sake as well. I wanted to make sure he knew this wasn't just about me and my needs—though, in truth, the session really *was* more about me. I needed to find some kind of peace.

Pops took it all. That shocked me, too, but it also led me to believe he was acknowledging that there was a problem—a problem with him and a problem between us. He was open to the idea of help, and in the short term his behavior changed. He drank less. As in the past, however, it didn't take long for him to return to his norm.

BELIEVE IT OR NOT, POPS STILL had the LeMans—we were now in the twenty-first century—but the car, too, had fallen on hard times. It had basically been on life support since the 1980s. Pops had revived it numerous times until, at one point in the 2000s, he just gave up. It was almost as if the car itself had finally begged for mercy.

The crazy thing was, not only did he still not get rid of the

LeMans—it was now parked, inoperable, in our driveway—but he kept paying insurance on it. Ryan and I would joke about it with Mom and Pops: "Why in the world are you guys wasting money on car insurance for a car that you're not even driving?" The expense was absurd. At the same time, it really bothered me to see the LeMans in that state: basically junked, the body rusting, the vinyl top water damaged. It had been the centerpiece of Pops's and my relationship throughout my childhood. Looking back now on his reluctance to let it go, I realize that it wasn't just about the car for either of us. It's what the LeMans represented: his attachment to his youth—and his attachment to his youth fueled my attachment to my youth. Maybe, for him, it was about an attachment to me as well? It might sound ridiculous to grieve a damn car, but I think that's what we were both doing. It had been such an essential part of who he was. He'd had the 'fro, the pick, the Newport hanging out of his mouth, the Budweiser, and the LeMans; the car was part of the costume. For me, as for Ryan, there were periods when it had been more present in our lives than Pops had been.

And still the LeMans had one more act. The county was cracking down on eyesores and public nuisances and had threatened to ticket Pops for having a rusted-out car that didn't run in the driveway. So he somehow pushed it into the backyard and left it there, acting out of some combination of stubbornness and sentimentality. My heart broke the first time I saw the LeMans out back. It was a real-life metaphor if ever there was one. Ryan and I used to talk about that: how the car's deterioration mirrored Pops's.

The final blow came literally in the mid-2000s, when a tree fell on the LeMans during a storm, leaving a huge dent in the roof. Still, it took a year of Pops's claiming, "Oh, I'm going to get it fixed," before he finally relented and had it towed away. I heard the news from Mom, so I didn't have a chance to say goodbye to the ancient green heap. If you had told me when I was a kid that I would one day mourn the LeMans's passing, man, I never would have believed you. Now I wish we still had the car so I could restore it. I'd love to have been able to pass it along to Del one day.

SOMEHOW POPS KEPT GOING INTO HIS sixties without ever changing his ways. Amazingly, between the drinking, the smoking, and the lousy diet, he never seemed to pay a price in terms of his health. (He had never set foot in a hospital as a patient until the bacterial pneumonia episode during the coronavirus pandemic.) He also never faced any serious consequences for drinking and driving. While he should've been pulled over more, he was ticketed for only two or three DUIs over the years—and consequently paid a ridiculous amount for car insurance. South Carolina's relatively lax drinking and driving laws were finally tightened in 2009. He did have his license suspended for a period, when Mom had to drive him around, which probably didn't improve their relationship. The cost of his car insurance skyrocketed even higher, but he never spent any time in jail—and somehow he never hurt anyone or himself. Ironically, it would be a car accident that led to his rebirth.

Jasmine's death, in 2012, like Grandma Rene's and Aunt Carrie Mae's, sent him on a further, deeper spiral. Life at home was already hard enough. Grandma Florence had moved in with my parents, her health declining to the point that she couldn't live by herself. It was the three of them—Pops, Mom, and Grandma—in that unhappy house, with Mom essentially serving as her mother's nurse. Then their granddaughter had fallen ill. That took a lot out of all of us, but Pops especially. He had been focused on Jasmine for six months, so on top of his grief, he felt unmoored, I think, by her death. He turned to drinking once again, with a vengeance.

His behavior became alarming, even for him. He started blacking out, experiencing periods when he couldn't remember whole conversations and large swaths of time. Mom would say that she and he would talk about something important, and then the next day when she referenced that discussion, he would respond, "What are you talking about?"

Mom grew concerned enough that she started mentioning these episodes to Ryan and me. In fact, it got to a point where Mom's stories about Pops blacking out became routine. It wasn't that Ryan and I didn't believe her, but she's been known sometimes to exaggerate things or overstate her case. That, coupled with the fact that Pops had always been a heavy drinker, made it difficult for us to discern how the episodes she was telling us about were different from the behavior he'd been displaying for the previous twenty years. She kept insisting that this was different, worse, and we started taking it seriously. Ryan, too, had some interaction with Pops where our father was just . . . *useless* is the best word I can come up with.

One afternoon in April 2018, he got into an accident while driving drunk. It was a relatively minor scrape, but it provided the impetus that finally changed his and my family's lives. The accident capped what had been a serious bender even by his standards. He had been downing beers pretty much nonstop the day and night before, and that morning as well. He left the house in his latest car, Grandma Florence's 1993 Honda Civic, and after parking and drinking with a buddy for a few hours, he drove over to a nearby Wendy's on Bush River Road, a major thoroughfare in our part of town, to get some food. He was leaving the parking lot when he sideswiped another car. Thankfully, neither he nor the other driver was hurt. She lived in our neighborhood and knew my family, so even though Pops was visibly intoxicated, she decided not to call the cops. Instead, she came by the house and told Mom what had happened. Between themselves, they managed to work out something to cover the damage, just like the incident with the rosebushes when I was a kid—and not unlike the time I almost became a teenage father. Betty Jo Melvin was a fixer of the highest order.

All the same, Ryan and I, our wives, Mom, Pops's nephews—we all came to realize it was finally time to stop enabling him.

When Mom called to tell me about the accident, I thought to myself, *Okay, this could be an opportunity*. She, Ryan, and I had several follow-up conversations and we all agreed we needed to get Pops into rehab. We couldn't just stage an intervention the next day, however. We were determined that, unlike our earlier attempt, we were going to make sure we knew what we were doing. We didn't want to blow what might be our last chance. One coincidence helped: my assistant at NBC had a stepfather whose friend had worked in the Obama White House and was an addiction specialist. He had started a nonprofit dedicated to the issue after his son, who had struggled mightily with addiction over the years, died by suicide. This man lives in the same town where I do. He and I had previously had lunch because he was interested in my doing a story on his group, or possibly getting involved on the fundraising side. He's a dynamic guy who's devoted to his family and to the causes he believes in. He and I spent a good portion of our lunch talking about his son, and what it was like to watch addiction cripple his kid and ultimately consume him—all of which struck a big chord with me. This father had done pretty well for himself in business, and after his son's death, he decided to devote the rest of his life to helping other families cope with addiction. In his dedication to that mission, he reminds me a lot of some of the fathers we've profiled in the "Dads Got This!" series, in particular Kevin Simmers, who founded the rehab clinic for women in Maryland, and Steven D'Achille, who set up the postpartum mental health center in Pittsburgh.

After Pops's accident, the guy from my town connected me with another addiction specialist. We had a conference call, and the two of them walked me through what my family needed to do, which included finding a certified counselor in Columbia who would come to Mom and Pops's house and facilitate the actual intervention.

I had only recently joined the *Today* show, and while a lot of these conversations were occurring, I was off on a multiday road trip with Al Roker, up the coast of Maine—one of what we call our "buddy trip" features. We went digging for clams, had a lobster bake, camped out, all for the show. But when we weren't filming, when Al and I were driving from site to site in a huge RV, I was working the phones: talking to the therapist we found in Columbia and trying to get Pops admitted into the rehab facility that we'd chosen. The pressure was weighing on me—the pressure of helping Pops, of course, but also of being on one of my first big *Today* show assignments. And so I confided in Al. He's so easygoing that I'm sure people spill their souls to him all the time. On that trip I certainly did, and he could not have been more gracious and helpful. At the time, I didn't know Al that well, but we've since become good friends. He told me recently, "I knew you were a good dude when, on that road trip, I could hear the conversations you were having with your family and the therapist." That's how our "bromance" started. Maybe not coincidentally, I see a lot of my dad in Al. Not the addiction—Al's never struggled with that—but the quality of being comfortable with who you are and not really conforming to society's standards in a lot of ways, and being perfectly fine with that. Al is also a lot like Jim Vance in that regard. A year later, after Pops's accident and our intervention, Lindsay threw me a blowout fortieth birthday party. One of my favorite pictures from the night is a photo of Pops, who was now in recovery, and Al Roker together. Al had said to me that night, "I want to make sure I meet your dad." When I introduced them, I was thinking, *Hey, this is kind of cool—my real dad and my work dad.*

OUR THERAPIST IN COLUMBIA INSISTED THAT we all have a session with her before she would facilitate an intervention with Pops. She specializes in treating alcohol addiction and had had some intimate experience dealing with it in her own family, so I felt we were in capable hands. I flew down for the meeting, which also included Ryan, Mom, my cousin Kevin, and his wife, Elaine. We sat in the therapist's office in downtown Columbia and went around the room taking turns speaking about Pops: why we were concerned, why we wanted him to get better. Nothing we were saying was new, but this time it felt different—purposeful. The therapist had clearly done this dozens if not hundreds of times, and she understood everything we were saying to her. She'd come up with a couple of recommendations for treatment facilities, which I had researched, and we had finally settled on Willingway Hospital in Statesboro, Georgia. After we all spoke our pieces, she told us how confronting Pops would go down.

We picked a date, a Sunday a few weeks away. The therapist told my mom to have a bag packed for Pops. Kevin and Elaine agreed to drive him to Statesboro, about two and a half hours from Columbia. We were each to write letters to my father and to read them to him. They weren't supposed to be long, just like a page in which we were to say how much he meant to us and what his alcoholism had stolen from us. We wrote about all his positive traits, and we shared memories. Kevin wrote about his mom, Carrie Mae, and how disappointed she would be if she were still alive and saw her brother in a state like his present one. Ryan and I shared childhood memories of Pops, and we both wrote about how we wanted our kids to have a grandfather because we hadn't—alcoholism had robbed us of both our grandfathers—and we knew Pops was capable of beating his addiction and being a terrific grandfather. Mom wrote a letter about wanting her husband back. It would be the first time that we had heard her say any of that not only out loud, in front of us, but to him.

The intervention took place at Ryan's house, in his den. Mom was worried Pops wouldn't come, but Ryan made it work. He drove over to their house around eleven in the morning and told Pops that he had promised the night before that he'd come over to Ryan's to help fix a door. It was a complete subterfuge, but Ryan figured Pops wouldn't remember what he had agreed to or not agreed to the previous evening, and Ryan was right. Pops shrugged and the two of them drove over to Ryan's, where the rest of us were waiting. Even though it was morning, our father was clearly on yet another bender; he was drunk and disheveled, but as soon as he walked in, he knew something was up, given that there was an older white lady he had never seen before, the therapist, sitting in Ryan's den. She started it off and she wasted no time—that was an important part of the approach. She didn't want to give Pops time to think about his decision; she didn't want to allow him any wiggle room for making up an excuse not to go. She had emphasized that with us a number of times: read your letter, move on to the next person. So we started reading and Pops sat there, and he listened and cried. We all did. When we finished, the therapist said, "Lawrence, there's a place in Georgia called Willingway that we think will help you and we want you to go. We've packed a bag, and Kevin and Elaine here, they're going to drive you to Statesboro right now."

I was fully prepared for him to say, "Hell no. Screw this." Or "I can do better here at home." Or "I'll change, I promise." He didn't.

Much to my surprise, much to everyone's surprise, he got up, hugged us, and shook some hands. He then said, "Okay, let's go," hopped in the back of Kevin and Elaine's SUV, and off they went to Georgia.

THE NEXT DAY, I CALLED WILLINGWAY to check in on Pops and found out why he had gone off so readily: he had been blackout drunk during our intervention. When he woke up the next day, he had no idea where he was or what had happened to him. It took him a couple of days to detox fully. But he stuck it out.

Willingway is a facility that doesn't allow cell phones and otherwise limits contact with the outside world. We couldn't speak to Pops directly, though we could talk to the treatment specialists and the therapists who were working with him to receive progress reports. We were also able to write him letters, and he had been given all the letters we had written him for the intervention, so he had those to go over when he came to and sobered up.

The first time I saw him again was well over a month into his treatment. There is a stage in Willingway's program, which adheres to an Alcoholics Anonymous model, where patients have to sit down one at a time, face-to-face with family members—it's part of the recovery process—so I flew down to Statesboro for a meet and greet with my newly sober father. I was anxious about it, but before I saw him, I had to meet with his therapists, who told me they were very pleased with his progress. He had been under a pretty hard-core regimen, with daily individual therapy sessions, group therapy sessions, and AA meetings. There was some socializing: all the patients ate together, and though they normally couldn't leave the grounds, they were allowed occasional field trips; while Pops was there, they went to a minor league baseball game. Physically, the place was attractive, not at all depressing or institutional. It's in a rural part of Southeast

Georgia, deliberately distanced from any major cities. The main building looks like an Adirondack lodge, and the grounds, while not spacious, were pretty and well-tended, with lawns and a creek and pond. It made me think of an old-school summer camp, the kind of place where rich kids go year after year to ride horses and have their first kisses. Oddly, it didn't look so different from the pictures I've seen of the Alderson Federal Prison Camp.

When I finally got to see Pops, we hugged and I knew almost instantly that he was a different person. He looked refreshed. He had a little pep in his step. He was happy to see me. He was social, engaged. As he showed me around, it was like he was the mayor of Willingway—everyone knew him; he knew everyone; he'd endeared himself to the staff. He was one of the older guys, but he seemed to get along with all ages and types, and it was a pretty heterogeneous group: young, old, men, women, black, white, gay, straight, alcoholics, drug addicts—they were all there together, beating their addictions.

Pops also had his sense of humor back. First he showed me where he had his AA meetings. Then he took me to his room, which was pleasant but fairly spartan, with just a few things in it: an AA book, some toiletries, a few other essentials. This was the first chance we'd had to be alone and really talk.

"Pops, how's it going in here?" I asked. "How you doing?"

"Man, let me tell you," he said. "I've got my problems, but you spend a few weeks in here listening to some of these people, you realize you're not that bad off. Some of these guys, they've tried to kill themselves. There are people in here on court order." He laughed. "I know I was bad off, but I don't think I was *this* bad off."

I had arrived at Willingway early, so we had breakfast together and I met some of his addict friends. I had the sense that he had forced some of these people to watch me on television when a few of them commented on how proud he was of me. People came up and said, "Hey! You must be Craig!" That made me feel great—not the attention, but the evidence of Pops's pride in me.

We then walked around the grounds and he told me about his treatment. We also played Frisbee golf—that was a new thing for both of us. All told, I was there for eight or nine hours. For me, it was an incredibly moving day—one I'll never forget. We hadn't spent a day together, just the two of us, since . . . I really had to stop and think on that one as I was writing. Probably since the time he'd come up by himself to D.C. when I was working there and I'd taken him to a Redskins game. The truth is, we hadn't spent a lot of good days together in the past couple decades. Bad days, sure, but not many good ones.

Leaving him was hard that afternoon. I was reminded of the story we'd done on Camp Grace, the program where kids got to go to camp with their dads in prison—a great opportunity to bond, but also heartbreakingly short.

POPS GOT OUT AFTER SOMEWHERE BETWEEN six and eight weeks. I wasn't able to get down to see him at home right away, but Ryan would keep me posted. Not only was Pops staying sober and going to his meetings; he was coming over to Ryan's house to hang out with the kids. He even went to a grandparents' day at Jayden's school with my mom. Pops showing up for a school program—that was almost unprecedented. And refreshing.

He was still smoking like a chimney, a pack a day, and he had started drinking nearly as much fully sugared soda as he once drank beer. Ryan and I used to have a running joke about never having seen Pops drink a glass of water, not even ice water on a hot day, and that's still probably true—though we'll take his new liquid vice over the old one. Exercise had never been a big part of Pops's life, and since he'd retired during Jasmine's illness, he'd grown even more sedentary. It was like we had done all this work to get him off alcohol so that sugar and tobacco could kill him.

Since he hadn't been to a doctor in several years, outside of Willingway, we finally got him to go in to see his regular internist for a complete physical. In our minds, he probably had early stage lung cancer or severe diabetes. It turned out he was in perfect health. I spoke to his doctor, who said that Pops may have had a little iron deficiency, but beyond that, no blood pressure issues, no high cholesterol, nothing. It was like sixty years of hard living had no effect on him. I hope I inherited that constitution.

The first time I saw him after Willingway was when I came down for an annual Melvin family vacation in Hilton Head, South Carolina. For a week we get a big house on the beach with six or seven bedrooms where we can all pile in. It's usually my family and Ryan's; Mom and Pops; Aunt Wanda and her daughter, Renee; Aunt Ella and Uncle Jake; my cousin Anita. We eat, we talk loud, we hang out, and we drink—not the way Pops used to drink, but booze is definitely a decent part of what we do that week.

Now, of course, we were concerned about drinking in front of Pops, and whether we might cause a relapse. We felt guilty about it. So before we got down to Hilton Head, Ryan and I talked things over and decided, "You know what? We'll bring a few bottles, whatever, but we'll just keep them in our rooms, not out in the common area where Pops might see." Once we got to the beach, that resolution may have lasted a day or two, until we realized Pops didn't care. One morning, in fact, we were at breakfast and he walked over holding a red Solo cup, his gait deliberately wobbly, and said, "Man, I just had to get a taste." Ryan and I must have looked aghast. He then burst out with a gleeful "I got you!" He really had.

For the whole trip he was engaged, fun, funny. He went swimming with the kids and rode bikes with them on the beach. That's something Ryan and I have no memories of: Pops ever riding a bicycle with either of us. We were watching him one day at the beach in his swim trunks, playing in the waves with his grandchildren, and we turned to each other and were both like, "Who *is* this guy?"

CHAPTER 8

"I'M HERE"

I wish I could say that Pops's sobriety has been a magic cure-all, that his not drinking has fixed our family's every problem. Life doesn't work that way, of course. We're incredibly proud of him, but at times he can still be antisocial. He still battles with what is likely depression.

But he's also opened up in ways that for him are remarkable. For instance, there was that day when Lindsay and I flew down to Spartanburg to see Lawrence, after his illness had reached its final stages, when he, Pops, Ryan, and I had spent that relaxed afternoon together, just hanging out. After we had said our goodbyes to Lawrence, we were all standing around in the yard for a bit, talking—Lindsay and me, Ryan, Pops, Angela, and her siblings, who had stopped by. Finally everyone exchanged hugs, and as Pops and I embraced, he told me, "Thank you." He meant for my having been there for Lawrence in the years since his diagnosis. It was a huge moment for both of us. My father is of that old-school disposition that feels there are certain things that should just be understood, accepted: but in that moment, with just those two words, he acknowledged his gratitude, out loud, intimately, and I received it.

Lindsay and I got into our car, waved goodbye to everyone, and headed off for the airport. Driving down the street, I noticed Pops walking up the sidewalk by himself, clearly lost in thought. It's hard to imagine what was going through his mind. When you have to bury a child and you know that for most of that child's life you weren't the kind of dad that you wanted to be, the kind of dad that your son needed . . . how do you come to terms with that?

The day after we returned home from Spartanburg, I saw I had a missed call from Pops. I called him back, and he said he just wanted to make sure that we had gotten back okay—*he* was checking on *me*! Then he said again, "Thank you." Just writing that makes me emotional. I needed that acknowledgment from him more than I had realized.

POPS'S SOBRIETY HAS IMPROVED MY PARENTS' marriage, but it's far from a fairy-tale happily ever after. Over the years they had both settled into roles that they maybe had gotten too comfortable with. In some ways it might have been easier for him always to be the bad guy and for her always to be the hero, but now that he's not the villain in the story anymore, it's been a little difficult for her to adjust to that—and maybe for him as well.

The flip side of their old dynamic, for me as their son, is that Pops has never been preachy as a parent—his occasional two- or three-sentence lectures aside. Betty Jo Melvin, on the other hand, is not shy about expressing her opinions. I'd like to think I've achieved a reasonable modicum of professional success and my personal life isn't in disarray, but when I talk to Mom sometimes, it's like I'm nine years old again. She's quick with the unsolicited advice. Not Pops—never. Maybe that was due in part to indifference and apathy; certainly some of it had to do with the addiction; but as I get older, I do wonder whether his approach wasn't deliberate. As someone who often felt like he was being judged, he never made me feel that way.

I have one memory on that score that may not seem like a big deal, but to me, in the moment, it was. In college, I had had a serious romance that turned disastrous. While I wanted things to work out, it was clear to me, and probably to her, that the relationship was coming to an end. I went home for a visit and I decided to talk to Pops about it. The circumstances were just too dark and messy and ugly to discuss with Mom, but I needed someone to confide in. Also, I felt like I had sort of let Pops down, because my girlfriend had become a part of our family for a couple of years—she had attended Aunt Carrie Mae's funeral—and he had actually liked her during a period of his life when he didn't much seem to like anyone. So I went back to the bedroom that had loomed so large throughout my childhood and poured out my heart to him. He didn't judge. He didn't chastise or offer advice. He simply listened. Finally, he said something like, "Oh, it's going to be all right. You'll be fine." That was it. The words weren't really important. His listening was what comforted me. I didn't entirely realize that then, as a twenty-year-old, but I do now, and I hope that insight is going to make me a better father. A lot of times when your children come to you with a problem, they don't really want advice; they just want you to hear them. I don't know if that was a conscious decision Pops made or if it was just his nature, but he got that. He always got that.

I'VE ENJOYED BEING ABLE TO CONNECT with so many different kinds of dads on so many different levels through my work on the *Today* show. One common thread I've found is that no matter how we were raised, we all want to do a little bit better than our dads did, and we then hope our kids will do a little bit better than we did. Give it a few more generations, and we're going to have a really impressive set of dads. Maybe the jokes will get better, too (which is itself kind of a dad joke).

I've seen that impulse in Pops. He certainly did better than his dad. He didn't abandon his family. He didn't just up and disappear and cut ties with his children. He stuck it out. He worked hard and met his responsibilities. While that may not seem particularly commendable from the vantage point of the 2020s, when we rightfully have much higher expectations for fathers, in the context of the early 1980s—especially considering what Pops had been through during his own childhood and the demons he had inherited—it was pretty honorable.

He had that work ethic that drove him to take extra shifts, work holidays, overtime, the third shift. Given my sometimes twelve- and thirteen-hour days at NBC, I think I may have inherited that from him . . . perhaps to a fault. He wanted to provide us with a life that he didn't have, and while I had it pretty good growing up, I'm trying to do the same for my kids, as is Lindsay. I do worry that we've possibly overachieved on that count. We live in a community that's a bit too idyllic, by a lot of measures, and in a home that may be a little too comfortable. I mean I had to listen to Del, at five, question the brand of Greek yogurt we stock. I tell him and Sibby all the time, "You two are living your best lives. It gets no better"—to the point that Sibby will now say, "Daddy, I'm living my best life!" The absurdity that is their childhoods!

I sometimes fear that my kids will grow up soft, that they won't be resilient because we haven't forced them to be resilient. Then again, as I'm writing this on an icy winter afternoon during the pandemic, I have a son upstairs who's still in his pajamas. This morning he announced, "I'm going to have a pajama day, Daddy." He's got school, though that means classes via Zoom for the time being. But still. . . . A couple of years ago, I might have gone to the mat on this. I might have said, "Nope. Sorry. We don't do pajama day. You brush your teeth and you put on clothes. We are part of a civilized society." But the longer I do this dad thing, the more I've come to a point where if no one's bleeding and the crying isn't above a certain decibel limit, I'm more or less okay with it. So when Del said he wanted a pajama day, I was like, "You know what? Why not?" I think of it this way: not getting dressed for Zoom class today will hardly keep him out of Harvard. But I'm not sure I have to justify it at all. Del felt validated and I avoided a fight. Surely there are times when "Why not?" is the wisest thing a parent can say.

For all his reticence, there is one piece of salient advice that Pops likes to give me: "Don't work too much. Don't miss out." It's a little ironic coming from him, but he knows whereof he speaks. Even with sobriety, he has had a hard time letting go of his guilt over all he missed as a dad, which troubles me. He, Ryan, and I have talked about it. Invariably any time when he's around and a conversation about our childhood or fatherhood comes up, he's compelled to apologize, sometimes profusely and emotionally. Even now. Even after the dozens of times we have told him, "Hey, we forgive you. We understand now that you were sick. You didn't know it then. We didn't really know it. But it's past." The problem is, he hasn't been able to forgive himself. I pray he reads this and does.

He has made peace with much of his past. When we were winding down one of our interviews, I asked Pops if he had anything he wanted to add. He surprised me by returning to the subject of his having been born in prison. "For a long time when I found out that I was a prison baby, man, that thing used to bother me. But one day I was sitting around thinking about it, I said, 'Shit, at least she had me.' And you know, it wasn't my doing I was born in prison."

"No regrets?" I asked.

"Nope. Not one bit. I'm here."

"No, I'm not talking about being born in prison. I just meant regrets about life in general. I mean, when you're seventy, you've got more years behind you than ahead of you."

"Well, everybody's got something they wish they'd done differently or whatnot." He returned to the topic of religion. "I kind of regret it, sometimes, that I should have been more of a churchgoer when you and Ryan were growing up. I guess it was the drinking and using the excuse of being tired or saying, 'I got to go to work' or 'I just came from work.' But you can't undo the things you missed out on. You just have to try to better yourself, to do better."

I hope he continues to take that to heart. For my part, even now, at the age of forty-two, I still yearn for his attention and approval. Not too long ago he and I were talking casually when he mentioned something about one of my broadcasts. "Wait, you watched that?" I asked, surprised. I knew he was proud of me, but I didn't think he paid that much attention to what I was doing on air. As I noted earlier, his taste in TV runs more to sports, of course, *Perry Mason* reruns, and Lifetime movies. But no, he was adamant. "Of course I watched it," he said. "I watch all your stuff." *Yeah, sure,* I thought. So I asked Mom and she said it was true. When I'm on, Pops is watching. Some days, depending on the news, I can be on for up to four hours, and, Mom told me, he will hang in there for the whole thing.

My chest swelled. There I was: a grown man with two kids of my own, a terrific marriage, and a job on network TV—and Pops had made my day by acknowledging me. I guess it's never too late.

ACKNOWLEDGMENTS

These pages that celebrate fatherhood, resilience, insecurity, faith, anger, transformation and so much more would not have been possible without a village of support and encouragement.

To my "Pops," thank you for being so willing to answer ALL of my questions honestly no matter how uncomfortable they made you. I sincerely hope and pray this book unburdens you and serves as a manual or guidebook of sorts for families ready to give up on a loved one for whatever the reason. Your story is going to do more good than you know. I promise.

To my mom, Betty Jo, talking and writing made me appreciate your sacrifices even more. For so many years, you were mother and father. You filled in all the gaps. From the beginning.

To my wife and champion, Lindsay, thank you for believing in me even when I wasn't so sure, prodding me to keep going, giving me the space and time to bring this to life, and for blessing us with Delano and Sybil, who inspired me to reflect and make all of it worthwhile. I love you.

To my man, Bruce Handy, who helped smooth the edges and breathe life into a deeply personal and emotional project, thank you for your patience and next level skill required to make everything I said and wrote so much better. Along with Mauro DiPreta at Harper-Collins, you two made it easier than I thought it would be.

Sloan Harris, thanks for talking me into exploring my soul and spirit over a glass of brown liquid magic a lifetime ago. Olivia, from the very beginning, you've helped make dreams come true.